Naookshelf

This series ⸺⸺⸺⸺⸺⸺⸺⸺ have many years'
experience an ⸺⸺⸺⸺⸺⸺⸺⸺⸺ ll
business. ⸺⸺⸺⸺⸺⸺⸺⸺⸺

If you are running a ⸺ business or are thinking of setting up your own business,
you have no time for the general, theoretical and often inessential detail of many
business and management books. You need practical, readily accessible, easy-to-
follow advice which relates to your own working environment and the problems
you encounter. The books on the NatWest Small Business Bookshelf fulfil these
needs.

- They concentrate on specific areas which are particularly problematic to the
small business.

- They adopt a step-by-step approach to the implementation of sound business
skills.

- They offer practical advice on how to tackle problems.

The authors

Peter Hall has conducted extensive research into franchising in the UK and Canada. He has worked as a manager and consultant in the music industry and is now employed by a merchant bank.

Rob Dixon is a lecturer in the Faculty of Business and Professional Studies at Newcastle Polytechnic and has authored a number of business books.

Other titles in this series

A Business Plan
Book-keeping and Accounting
Exporting
Hiring and Firing
Managing Growth
Retailing
Selling
Small Business Survival
Starting Up

NatWest Small Business Bookshelf

Franchising

Peter Hall and **Rob Dixon**

Pitman Publishing
128 Long Acre, London WC2E 9AN
A Division of Longman Group UK Limited

First published in Great Britain, 1988. Revised edition published in association with the
National Westminster Bank, 1989

© Longman Group UK Ltd 1988, 1989

British Library Cataloguing in Publication Data

Hall, Peter
   Franchising.
   1. Great Britain. Franchising
   I. Title   II. Dixon, R. (Robert)
   658.8′708′0941

ISBN 0-273-03144-9

Typeset, printed and bound in Great Britain.

Contents

Preface

Franchising is intended to be a concise, easy-to-read, explanatory book of the questions that are most commonly raised by each party in a franchise agreement. Unnecessary technical detail has been omitted wherever possible in order to ensure that the book is readily comprehensible to the layman. The text assumes that the reader has little or no prior knowledge of the franchising industry.

The masculine gender has been used throughout when referring to the franchisee – this is not meant to be discriminatory but is in the interests of brevity. Similarly, the franchisor is often referred to as 'he', although in practice 'he' will almost invariably be a limited company. Once again this approach has been adopted merely to improve the flow of text.

Peter Hall
Rob Dixon
Spring 1989

Acknowledgements

Grateful thanks are given to Ray Leach, Franchise Manager at NatWest, and Charlotte Ridings for their help with the revisions in this new edition.

Special gratitude must be expressed to Mike and Maureen Hall for making this and so many other things possible. Their unwavering help and support is deeply appreciated. Thanks go to Jill and Laura Dixon who had great patience even without knowing it.

1 What is franchising?

What is franchising? □ The elements of franchise agreements □ The history of franchising □ Early developments in the US □ Franchising in the 1950s and 1960s □ Franchising from the 1970s to the present day □ General reasons for the growth of franchising □ The economic importance of franchising

Franchising can best be described as a system of distribution whereby one party (the franchisor) grants to a second party (the franchisee) the right to distribute products, or perform services, and to operate a business in accordance with an established marketing system. The franchisor provides the franchisee with expertise, trade marks, the corporate image, and both initial and ongoing support, in return for which the franchisee pays to the franchisor certain fees. The objective is that both parties benefit from each other.

The benefits to the franchisee include:

- the goodwill that the franchisor has developed
- the management and marketing expertise offered by the franchisor
- reduced cost of sales as a result of centralized bulk purchasing by the franchisor on behalf of all franchisees in the chain.

The franchisor benefits from:

- the motivation of a self-employed franchisee (as opposed to a hired manager)
- the rapid expansion of a chain of outlets for his products without having to provide all the required capital himself (since the franchisees supply the capital needed for their individual outlets)
- the franchisees' knowledge of the local market.

What is franchising?

Many different definitions of franchising have been offered over the years by different authors. This diversity is due in part to the fact that franchising covers a very broad range of businesses. Some definitions are very general and try to include all possible types of franchise, while others are more specific and give a much more precise definition of a particular type of franchise but will not necessarily be broad enough to cover all aspects of the franchise industry.

The British Franchise Association (the BFA) – the UK franchise industry's trade organization – has proposed the following definition of franchising:

'A franchise is a contractual licence granted by one person (the franchisor) to another (the franchisee) which:

(*a*) permits or requires the franchisee to carry on during the period of the franchise a particular business under or using a specified name belonging to or associated with the franchisor; and

(*b*) entitles the franchisor to exercise continuing control during the period of the franchise over the manner in which the franchisee carries on the business which is the subject of the franchise; and

(*c*) obliges the franchisor to provide the franchisee with assistance in carrying on the business which is the subject of the franchise (in relation to the organization of the franchisee's business, the training of staff, merchandising, management or otherwise); and

(*d*) requires the franchisee periodically during the period of the franchise to pay to the franchisor sums of money in consideration for the franchise or for goods or services provided by the franchisor to the franchisee; and

(*e*) which is not a transaction between a holding company and its subsidiary (as defined in s.154 of the Companies Act 1948) or between subsidiaries of the same holding company or between an individual and a company controlled by him.'

(NB clause (*e*) establishes the difference between a franchise and an agency agreement.)

While the BFA definition is one of the most detailed definitions of franchising, it still fails to mention certain basic elements of most franchise agreements including the following points:

● Before the business concept is offered as a franchise the franchisor should thoroughly test its suitability for franchising by setting up and operating at least one (and preferably several) company-owned pilot outlets. These should be operated using exactly the same systems and methods as those that the franchisees will be required to use. It is also important that they are operated under similar market conditions as those that the franchisees will face.

- In addition to the continuing management services fee referred to in section (*d*) of the definition, the franchisee will almost certainly be required to pay an initial fee (often referred to as a 'front-end' fee). This initial fee is partly in consideration for initial training and assistance provided by the franchisor before the franchisee's outlet is opened.
- A key feature of franchising is that the franchisee owns his own business – it is not owned by the franchisor. Thus the franchisee is an independent businessman in his own right. Franchising is a symbiotic relationship – the franchisor and franchisee depend heavily upon each other, yet at the same time they remain legally independent of one another (as opposed to an agency agreement whereby representations made by the agent become binding upon the principal and therefore the two parties are not legally independent).

The elements of franchise agreements

Because of the broad scope of franchising it is very difficult to come up with a definition which will be suitable in all situations. However, the basic elements of nearly all franchise agreements (particularly 'business format' franchises) can be summarized by the following features:

- The franchisor owns a unique product, piece of equipment, or method of operation along with a business name and image and the associated goodwill.
- The franchisor tests the proposed franchise operation in the marketplace by operating pilot outlets in order to ensure that the operation will be suitable for franchising.
- The franchisor grants to the franchisee a licence permitting him to trade under the franchisor's name and to use those products, equipment, or processes.
- The terms of the agreement must be comprehensively described in a franchise contract which should include all methods of operation to which the franchisee must adhere, the obligations of the franchisor, the geographical area within which the franchisee has the right to operate, etc.
- Before the franchisee opens his outlet he will be fully trained by the franchisor in all aspects of the operation. Once the outlet is in operation the franchisor will have a continuing obligation to the franchisee to provide assistance, support and advice.
- The franchisor exerts continuing control over the franchisee in order to ensure that the stipulated methods of operation are adhered to throughout the duration of the franchise agreement.

- In consideration for the initial and ongoing assistance and the use of the franchisor's name, goodwill, etc. the franchisee will usually pay both initial and continuing fees (which constitute the franchisor's income).
- The franchisee is an independent businessman and must own his outlet. He must be prepared to make a substantial investment in his business from his own personal resources.

The history of franchising

The word 'franchise' is derived from the French verb 'franchir' and the more modern verb 'affranchir', both meaning 'to free' (used in this context to express freedom from servitude or restraint).

Contrary to popular belief, franchising is not an American invention – it first emerged in Britain during the Middle Ages when certain powerful nobles would pay a lump sum to the Government and would agree to provide continuing personal support and services in return for the right (i.e. the franchise) to collect local taxes.

Franchising resurfaced in the eighteenth and nineteenth centuries when the long-term right to a monopoly in some form of trade or commerce would be granted either by a legislative body or by royalty to a franchisee. As consideration for the granting of this right, the franchisee would make an initial cash payment and would also have certain continuing obligations to the franchisor.

The next major step in the history of franchising came with the 'tied house' agreements between breweries and landlords which developed during the eighteenth century and which still exist today. During the 1700s there was a period of growing concern over the increasing social problems resulting from the widespread availability of alcohol. Legislation was therefore introduced in order to regulate the sale of beer and spirits. Public houses were now required to hold a liquor licence in order to be allowed to sell alcohol. Since only a restricted number of licences were granted, the value of those inns which were successful in obtaining these licences rapidly rose. Consequently many prospective landlords found that they simply could not afford to purchase hostelries. The breweries therefore stepped in and started buying the licensed premises themselves and leasing them to the publicans. As part of the agreement the publican would undertake to sell exclusively beer made by that brewery. The legislation also required that the standard of many of the existing inns be improved considerably, so the breweries offered to finance the required improvements in many hostelries independently owned in return for which the landlords would agree to a tying arrangement.

Early developments in the US

The development of franchising in the US can perhaps serve as a useful indicator for industries in the UK of how businesses can be spread using franchising. Franchising first emerged in the United States when the automobile manufacturers realized that franchised rather than company-owned dealerships made excellent economic sense for several reasons, including:

- The amount of capital needed to set up a national distribution network would be immense. By using a franchised network the manufacturers did not have to provide this capital themselves.
- Franchisees would initially absorb any strong fluctuations in retail prices. The manufacturers would have to absorb all these costs themselves if they sold through company-owned outlets.
- Franchisees would also absorb a proportion of the costs of overproduction and styling errors made by the manufacturers.
- The manufacturers would be freed from the problems of disposing of second-hand cars traded in against new purchases.

By granting exclusive territories to franchisees the automobile manufacturers were able to assure dealers that they would be protected from competition from other dealers selling the same model. This meant that the manufacturers were able to attract a high standard of franchisee. Furthermore, by limiting the number of outlets within a given territory the manufacturers could ensure a large sales volume for each franchisee. Therefore, like the breweries under the tied house system, they could insist that the dealers sold only their models and not those of other manufacturers. In return for exclusive territories the franchisor could also demand that each franchisee make adequate investments in premises, stocks of vehicles, equipment needed for good after-sales service etc., thereby maintaining and improving the corporate image and the standards required by the manufacturer. Of course, these benefits might have been achieved equally well by using manufacturer-owned outlets rather than franchises but, as already stated, the manufacturers would have then had to raise massive amounts of capital themselves in order to set up an adequate nationwide network of outlets for their cars. Under the franchise system this capital was provided by the franchisees rather than the manufacturers.

The franchised form of car dealership was fully established by 1910 and is still predominant today. It is estimated that 95 per cent of new passenger car sales in the United States are made through franchised outlets.

The second major industry to employ the franchise method of distribution was the soft drinks bottling industry. Developing around the turn of the twentieth century, the franchisee would be granted the right to use the packaging and brand name of the franchisor, from whom he would buy the concentrated syrup from which the final product was made.

When setting up a distribution network a soft drinks manufacturer must consider two factors which dictate what is the most appropriate structure for the network. Firstly, it is highly uneconomic to ship the final product over long distances since it is extremely bulky in terms of both its high water content and the bottles in which the final product is sold. Therefore the most feasible method of distribution is to use many localized bottling plants where the drink is made up from the concentrated syrup rather than having one large centralized plant. Secondly, the use of a returnable bottle with a refundable deposit limits the profitable radius of distribution of bottled drinks from any one site. This factor also suggests the use of many localized sites rather than one centralized plant. However, setting up many plants requires a great deal of capital and therefore franchising is an attractive proposition as it reduces the level of finance that the manufacturer must invest in the distribution network. For these reasons franchised bottling plants are used by nearly all the major soft drinks manufacturers including Coca Cola, Pepsi Cola, 7-Up, etc.

The third major industry to employ the franchise method of distribution was the petrol industry. The majority of petrol stations were initially owned by the oil companies themselves. However, during the petrol price wars of the 1930s the independent stations were found to have an advantage over the company-owned outlets because they had greater flexibility in setting prices at the appropriate competitive level on a local basis. The company-owned outlets were disadvantaged because central management was unable to set competitive prices in each and every area across the country. This resulted in declining profitability for the oil companies who therefore decided to franchise their stations in order to obtain the benefits of the flexibility of the independents while still maintaining a standardized corporate image right across the country. As a result, not only did the sales of petrol significantly increase, but the oil companies also started to receive large amounts of rental income from the franchisees since they retained control of the premises used in the nationwide franchise network.

The three types of franchises outlined above, i.e. the car dealerships, soft drinks bottlers and petrol stations, have become known as 'traditional' or 'first generation' franchises. Traditional franchises account for a large proportion of the total revenues generated through franchised outlets.

The fourth major development in franchising in the United States was the emergence of franchised wholesaler-retailer chains in the 1920s and

1930s. These were formed in response to the ever increasing expansion of corporate chains which began to squeeze out the independent retailers. The franchised chains allowed small retailers to enjoy the benefits of discounts obtained through bulk purchasing by the wholesaler plus the benefit of the image of a large chain, while at the same time retaining the flexibility of an independent. The 1930s also saw the start of the growth in popularity and importance of shopping malls in the United States. The lease requirements of many of these malls excluded many of the smaller independent retails who were regarded by the property developers as being high risk tenants since they faced a high probability of failure within the first few years of starting up. This was another reason for the growth in popularity of franchised chains as the franchisors were usually large enough to be able to satisfy these lease requirements and therefore gain access to the all-important shopping malls.

Franchising in the 1950s and 1960s

The next major advance in the field of franchising came with the growth in prominence of 'business format' (or 'second generation') franchises in the US during the 1950s and in the UK during the 1960s. Business format franchising is now the most important growth area within the franchising industry.

Unfortunately the image of the UK franchise industry as as a whole suffered during the 1960s as a result of fraudulent operators who were involved in pyramid selling schemes. Consequently its popularity dwindled as the public erroneously confused pyramid selling and franchising. In the United States the franchising 'boom' (which was fuelled by sales of business format franchises) only lasted as long as the bull market of the 1960s. When the stock market went into decline in 1969 the expansion of franchising temporarily levelled out.

Franchising from the 1970s to the present day

A second period of rapid expansion in the franchising industry emerged in the UK in the early 1980s. This process was aided in Britain by the formation by eight of the reputable franchise companies in December 1977 of the British Franchise Association. The main objective behind the formation of the BFA was to lend an air of respectability to the franchise industry by imposing a code of ethical conduct upon franchisors who were admitted to membership. The BFA represented a group of franchisors which the public could trust as being reputable and also served as a source of information for anybody interested in franchising and as a promotional body for the industry as a whole. It was hoped that the existence of such a body would help to dispel the idea that had developed during the era of pyramid selling that all franchisors were fraudsters who, having secured an initial downpayment from unsuspecting franchisees, would hastily disappear, never to be seen again.

General reasons for the growth of franchising

Role of service activities

This is possibly the most important environmental factor responsible for the rapid growth of the franchising industry in recent years. Many service industries are relatively personnel-intensive and they often rely on a distribution network consisting of a large number of outlets dispersed over a relatively large geographical area. The franchising technique is particularly suitable for this type of operation as it offers considerable advantages in terms of staff motivation, and may also reduce some of the problems associated with controlling local management from a remote head-office. Changing life-styles, such as the increasing number of women going out to work, and the greater leisure time and affluence enjoyed in the West, have resulted in a growing demand for services such as fast-food restaurants, home cleaning and maintenance services, car maintenance services, etc. In short, the social and economic environment has become increasingly conducive to the emergence of a great variety of franchises.

Value placed on self-employment

The increased value that society currently places on self-employment has also encouraged the growth of franchising. Entrepreneurialism is viewed in a very favourable light, and a high level of self-esteem and social acknowledgement can be gained through self-employment. As a result, an increasing number of people are experiencing the desire to escape the bureaucratic environment of the large organization and to 'go it alone' by starting their own small business. Many studies have shown that there is indeed a widespread desire amongst ordinary workers to run their own business. Unfortunately, most of these would-be entrepreneurs lack either the necessary skills or the confidence to set up a totally independent business. However, the franchising system overcomes many of the problems commonly associated with starting a business, and thereby provides a much easier route to self-employment and the social esteem that goes with it. The extent of the social value that is placed on entrepreneurialism can be seen in many of the adverts that are often used to sell franchises. These adverts tend to emphasize the social and psychological benefits of 'being your own boss' just as much as the potential financial rewards. So long as society continues to place a value on being self-employed then franchising can be expected to continue to grow.

Unemployment

Whilst many people are attracted to self-employment as a means of escaping the frustrations of employee status, other less fortunate individuals are forced to consider starting their own business because there seems to be little prospect of securing any other form of employment. During the recent economic recession many people have been made redundant, only to discover that, for whatever reason, they are unable to find further employment. Many of these people have therefore turned to self-employment, possibly using their redundancy payment as capital. Franchising may be an alternative for many of these people as they may lack the necessary 'human capital' (i.e. the skills and knowledge) to start a totally independent venture, although there are doubts as to whether or not they make the best franchisees.

Availability of finance

The growth of franchising has also been helped by the increase in recent years in the availability of finance on more attractive terms than are usually offered to independent small businesses. Banks have developed special arrangements specifically designed to provide suitable funding for franchisees. Furthermore the City has warmed to franchising and a number of franchisors have been successfully floated on the Stock Market. The growing involvement of the banks and financial institutions has proved to be a key element in the expansion of franchising, and has generally helped to increase the profile and respectability of the industry as a whole.

The economic importance of franchising

Turnover

Unfortunately very little statistical research into franchising has been conducted in the UK but the most accurate commentary on the size, scale and character of franchising is contained within the series of annual surveys produced on behalf of the British Franchise Association under

National Westminster Bank sponsorship. The problem of different definitions of franchising makes comparisons between both different countries and different time periods hazardous. For example, sales achieved through 'traditional' franchises are usually included in American statistics but are often excluded from European statistics. Consequently any quoted figures should be used with caution. However, while specific statistics may differ there can be no doubt that the franchising sector has enjoyed phenomenal growth in the UK in recent years. Turnover through business format franchises has increased from approximately £670 million in 1981 to approximately £3800 million in 1988, far outstripping the relative growth in gross domestic product over the same period. There were believed to be approximately 250 business format franchises in the UK in 1988 and turnover is forecast to increase to £10 000 million by 1993.

Employment

Franchising has also made an increasing contribution to employment. The number of business format franchisees in the UK has more than doubled from nearly 8000 in 1984 to 16000 in 1988. The number of people employed in these franchised outlets has risen to 181 500, including those people employed in supplying the franchise industry. What is particularly significant is that many franchisees state that they would never have entered self-employment had it not been for the franchise concept. Thus franchising is seen as providing an excellent route into self-employment – a consideration which is particularly important in view of the current unemployment figures and the value that is placed on self-employment and entrepreneurship in the prevailing social and economic environment.

Business failure

A further economic benefit offered by franchising is the reduced likelihood of failure. Business failure affects the economy as a whole and anyone who buys or sells in the market-place is potentially affected by it. Suppliers are directly affected as they suffer the cost of uncollectable debts owed by failed businesses. Customers are also indirectly affected as, for example, higher interest charges which are levied by lenders in order to compensate them for the increased risk of non-repayment are passed on to the ultimate consumer in the form of higher selling prices. It is often suggested that whereas 90 per cent of independent businesses fail within five years of start-up, only 12–14 per cent of franchisees fail over the same period. (The BFA estimates that only 2 per cent of franchisees of its member companies fail.)

Clearly franchising has much to offer our economy. The areas in which franchising already plays an extremely important role include food and drink, home maintenance, business services, vehicle maintenance, leisure, clothing, health and beauty and transport. As the number and range of franchises further develops, this method of business will assume increasing economic importance in terms of turnover, market share and employment.

2 Types of franchise and franchisee

Licences □ Distributorships (or 'dealerships') □ 'Agents' and 'distributors' □ Right to use a trade mark □ Concessions □ Business format franchises □ Franchisor's input □ Basic elements of business format franchises □ Area franchisees □ Multiple franchisees

Many different forms of agreements are regularly and loosely described as 'franchises'. The most common examples include:

- Licences
- Distributorships/dealerships
- Right to use trade mark
- Concessions
- Business format franchises

This book is primarily concerned with business format franchises, but reference is made to other arrangements for the sake of completeness.

Licences

A licensing agreement can be defined as one which confers on the licensee the right to manufacture, sell, or use something which is the exclusive property of the licensor. The licence agreement, which will last for a stated period, may stipulate an exclusive territory in which the licensee can exercise this right.

The licensee and licensor are legally independent of each other. Consequently the licensor usually has little or no control over the licensee beyond the requirement that he complies with the stipulated specifications for the manufacture and sale of the product (such as content and quality, etc.).

In consideration for the licence the licensee pays the licensor a royalty on sales of the licensed product. An example of a licence is a soft drinks bottling agreement.

Distributorships (or 'dealerships')

A distributorship is an agreement whereby one party (the manufacturer) grants to a second party (the distributor) the right to sell the manufacturer's products within a given area. In return for the exclusive rights to a specific territory and the right to operate under the manufacturer's trade mark, thereby benefiting from the manufacturer's promotional effort, the distributor will be required to maintain the standards and corporate image demanded by the manufacturer and will often be required to hold at least some minimum level of stock. The distributor may also be required to commit himself exclusively to the manufacturer's products. The classic examples of a distributorship arrangement include car dealerships and the operation of franchised petrol stations.

2

'Agents' and 'distributors'

The terms 'distributor' and 'agent' are often incorrectly used synonymously. In fact the two terms have quite different legal meanings. An agent is a person who has the authority (either expressly or impliedly) to act on behalf of another person or company (the 'principal'). As far as a third party, such as a customer, who is dealing with the agent is concerned there is no obvious legal distinction between the agent and the principal. Consequently the actions of the agent, and any representations made by him, are legally binding upon the principal. One of the fundamental requirements of a franchise is that the franchisee and franchisor are indeed legally independent and therefore agency agreements fall outside the definition of a franchise. Under a distributorship agreement the two parties are legally independent and therefore such an agreement can be considered a franchise in its loosest sense.

Most franchise agreements include a clear statement that the franchisee is not an agent (or a partner) of the franchisor, and that the franchisee has no authority to represent himself as being the franchisor's agent. Some franchise contracts go so far as to require the franchisee to display a statement to this effect in his business premises in order that customers of the franchisee will be aware of the fact that the franchisor and franchisee are legally independent of one another. Thus the franchisor cannot be held responsible for the franchisee's actions or representations. Clearly it is important to recognize the difference between an agency agreement and a 'franchise' contract such as a dealership.

Right to use a trade mark

A trade mark is defined in the Trade Marks Act 1938 s.68(1) as:

'... a mark used or proposed to be used in relation to goods for the
purpose of indicating, or so as to indicate, a connection in the course of
a trade between the goods and some person having the right either as
proprietor or as registered user to use the mark'.

The franchisor grants to the franchisee the right to exploit commer-
cially a trade mark, in return for which the franchisee will periodically pay
to the franchisor certain fees.

The franchisor retains ownership of the trade mark and any goodwill
associated with that trade mark accrues to the franchisor rather than to the
franchisee. Consequently the control involved in the continuing relationship between the two parties is absolutely crucial in order to maintain this
goodwill. The franchisor exercises this control by stipulating the exact
method of manufacture of the product, acceptable means of promotion etc.

Concessions

A concession can take one of two forms:

(a) The franchisor grants to the franchisee the right to trade in a given
location. One of the most common examples of this sort of concession is
the franchising of catering rights for a motorway service area, or in an
airport. In return for this right the franchisee will usually pay both an
initial fee and continuing management services fees
(b) The franchisor grants the right to sell a particular product or range
of products within an existing retail outlet. Concessions such as these are
granted in many department stores in return for management services
fees on turnover.

All the franchise methods mentioned so far can be grouped together
under the title 'traditional' or 'first generation' franchises.

Business format franchises

First generation franchises are undoubtedly important means of product
distribution. Nevertheless, when people use the term 'franchise' they are

more often than not referring to what has become known as the 'business format' or 'second generation' franchise.

Business format franchises fall into three broad categories mainly distinguished by the level of investment needed from the franchisee. The categories are:

- the 'job' franchise
- the 'business' franchise
- the 'investment' franchise

Job franchises

Job franchises require a fairly minimal financial investment by the franchisee, and can usually be operated from the franchisee's home. The largest part of the total investment may be, say, the purchase price of a van. The term 'job' franchise derives from the fact that the franchisee is in effect buying himself a job. One-man operations which do not require business premises such as domestic maintenance services (e.g. household cleaning, drain clearance etc.) and mobile vehicle servicing are ideal for job franchising.

Business franchises

'Business' franchises require a much larger investment in stocks, equipment and business premises. Because the scale of operation is much larger than that of a job franchise the franchisee will normally be unable to run the business on his own and will usually have to employ additional staff (possibly only on a part-time basis) in order to operate effectively. The range of business franchises is vast, and includes photocopying and printing services, picture framing, business services (such as accounting), dry-cleaning and take-away foods.

Investment franchises

'Investment' franchises require a relatively large investment by the franchisee, often in excess of £200000. Franchisees who undertake investment franchises are concerned primarily with earning a return on their capital investment rather than with providing themselves with employment. One example of an investment franchise is a franchised hotel. Many of the fast-food outlets also require such a large amount of capital that they are considered to be investment rather than business franchises, although there can be no precise dividing line between an investment and a business franchise.

Franchisor's input

Under most business format franchises, regardless of whether they are
job, business or investment franchises, the franchisee is provided with a
total business package. This consists of:

- initial training in all aspects of running the business
- trade marks
- logos
- standard design for the layout and appearance of any premises
- standard furnishings and colour schemes
- continuous ongoing advice and assistance.

The franchisor will lay down rules for exactly how the business is to be run,
including:

- opening hours
- pricing policy
- quality of service
- sources of supply
- hiring and training practices.

In short, the franchisor retains control over virtually every single aspect of
the franchisee's operation. The level of control exerted by the franchisor
is so great that in most cases the franchisee need not have had any prior
experience in that particular field of business because he will be fully
trained by the franchisor. All he has to do is to follow the rules laid down
by the franchisor and demonstrate the necessary personal commitment
and effort.

Basic elements of business format franchises

The basic elements of most 'business format' franchise agreements can be
summarized by the following features:

- A detailed contract will contain all the terms and conditions relating to
  the operation of the franchise and the obligations of both parties.
- The franchisee is allowed to operate in a defined territory (which may
  or may not be exclusive) for a specified period using the franchisor's
  trade name, logo, processes etc.
- The franchisor provides an entire business concept, covering all aspects
  of the operation. All procedures will be laid down in an 'operating

manual'. The franchisee must adhere to these procedures in order to ensure standardization of products and service offered in all units.

- The business format which is offered by the franchisor will usually have been tried and tested through operation of franchisor-owned pilot outlets, and will have been proved to be successful before the concept is sold as a franchise.
- Before a franchisee opens his outlet and commences trading he will be fully trained in all aspects of the operation of the business by the franchisor.
- The franchisor will continue to support and assist the franchisee once the business is in operation. This support will include all back-up services such as advertising and promotion of both the franchise chain as a whole, and of each franchisee's individual outlet.
- The franchisee will benefit from the goodwill which has been built up by the franchisor.
- In consideration for the rights granted by the franchisor, and the initial training and ongoing assistance which were provided, the franchisee will pay to the franchisor both an initial fee and continuing management services fees. He will also be required to make a contribution to an advertising fund in order to pay for national and local promotion.
- The franchisor will require the franchisee to make a significant financial investment in the business from his personal resources and will also expect the franchisee to take an active role in the day-to-day operation of the outlet.
- The franchisee will own the business and be legally independent of the franchisor. He will also be free to dispose of his business (subject to certain conditions such as first right of refusal by the franchisor, and vetting of prospective purchasers by the franchisor in order to ensure that they are suitable franchisees).
- All franchised units will, as far as possible, be identical in terms of appearance and the services which are offered. Consequently the public will perceive each outlet as being part of a larger chain.

There are literally thousands of business format franchises covering an incredible range of businesses. Some of the more unusual business format franchises that have appeared in the United States include one whereby franchisees were set up in business and granted exclusive rights to pick up dead bodies washed up along certain stretches of the California coastline, and a mobile dog grooming system including a bath tub in the back of a van!

Occasionally an existing independent businessman is persuaded by a franchisor operating in the same industry to convert his business into a franchised outlet. The franchisor contributes his trade mark and operating systems, while the new franchisee contributes his property, expertise and goodwill to the franchisor's chain.

Converting existing businesses into part of a franchise chain is becoming increasingly common in the UK. Examples include independent estate agencies and travel agencies becoming part of a franchised chain.

Area franchisees

An area franchise involves the sale by the original franchisor of the exclusive franchise rights in a given territory to an 'area franchisee'. The area franchisee then either opens and operates the franchised units himself, or he sub-franchises units within that area to other franchisees.

Area franchising is much more predominant in North America than in the UK. This is perhaps due to the vast difference in the geographical size. There is less merit in having area franchises in a small country such as the UK than in large countries. There are also legal problems for systems with built in sub-franchising arrangements, due to the earlier pyramid selling schemes. Many American and Canadian franchisors see area franchising as an essential policy in order to ensure adequate nationwide control of outlets, and also as the best means of taking into account the large differences in consumer profiles and tastes in different parts of the country. For example, the Canadian province of Quebec is largely French speaking, and as a market is as different to, say, Ontario as France is to Britain.

The major application of area franchising in the UK arises from foreign franchisors selling the right to open franchised outlets in the UK to a master franchisor. British franchises may also be established abroad through area franchising.

Franchising an area

The down payment for the territory may be determined on a per capita basis, i.e. the fee paid by the area franchisee will be based on the size of the population resident within the defined territory. If the area franchisee subsequently sub-franchises outlets to individual franchises then the original franchisor might take some proportion of the 'front-end' fees collected by the area franchisee, and will also receive some proportion (often approximately one-quarter) of the management services fee on turnover paid by individual franchisees to the area franchisee.

Alternatively, a territory can be bought as a block of franchises. For example, it may be estimated that a territory can support fifty franchised outlets, so the area franchisee buys the rights to all of these units by making a down payment on each one. The balance on each outlet then becomes payable if and when it opens.

The area franchisee is responsible for achieving the sales performance target set for his territory, and will therefore seek out prospective franchisees, since the area franchise agreement can usually be terminated if the area franchisee fails to open outlets according to a predetermined plan. In some cases the original franchisor will reserve the right to make the final selection of individual sub-franchisees. Once a sub-franchisee has been selected then the area franchisee will be responsible for providing training and support. He is also responsible for ensuring that the quality standards set by the original franchisor are maintained by the individual franchisees in his territory.

The benefits of area franchising

- It allows rapid growth and expansion of the franchise chain throughout the country and in foreign territories.
- The area franchisee will have a much better knowledge than the original franchisor of specific market conditions and consumer tastes within a given territory.
- It results in less administration for the original franchisor who has to deal with fewer franchisees. Furthermore, the area franchisees will usually be more sophisticated than individual sub-franchisees – this should make the original franchisor's job easier.

The disadvantages of area franchising

- Lower income for the original franchisor – the total management services fee received on sales may be as low as only 15 per cent of that which would be received from a similar franchisee who is not operating in an area which is controlled by an area franchisee (NB the original franchisor will usually collect the majority of the advertising fee which is levied on sales, in order to finance national advertising).
- It may be difficult to find and train area franchisees who fully understand and adopt the objectives of the original franchisor. The area franchise agreement may last for 20 years, but the area franchisee may have turned out to be unsuitable from the original franchisor's point of view within the first couple of years. It may be very expensive (or even impossible) for the original franchisor to terminate the area franchise contract.
- One of the biggest problems for the original franchisor is the potential loss of corporate reputation if the area franchisee fails to maintain the

required standards. For example, McDonald's Corporation recently won a legal battle in France after the area franchise owner almost ruined the reputation of the main company by serving hamburgers that did not taste even remotely like those sold in other countries.

A common feature associated with area franchise programmes is that after the area franchisee has fully developed the territory, the original franchisor will often offer to buy back the area franchise agreement. This implies that area franchising is possibly viewed primarily as a method of achieving an extremely rapid rate of development and expansion of the chain. Once the required geographical coverage has been achieved in the minimum time period, the disadvantages of area franchising to the original franchisor may appear to outweigh the advantages.

Multiple franchises

The franchisee is usually thought of as an individual businessman owning and running on a day-to-day basis a single small outlet. However, franchises are increasingly being bought by companies which may own many franchised outlets without being actively involved in the day-to-day running of any of them. Such franchisees are often referred to as 'multiple franchisees', as opposed to the small businessman described above who is often called a 'single' franchisee (even though he may own more than one outlet).

The main features which distinguish a multiple from a single franchisee are:

- The multiple franchisee will make more use of hired managers, and will not be actively involved in the day-to-day management of individual outlets, whereas the single franchisee will often have bought the franchise with the primary objective of providing himself with employment.
- The multiple franchisee will usually have a much larger financial investment in the franchise system.
- The multiple franchisee will often maintain other business interests apart from his franchises.

Multiple franchisees are usually primarily interested in franchising either purely as an investment opportunity for 'spare' financial resources, or as a means of diversification. The single franchisee on the other hand is primarily interested in providing himself with employment and a personal income.

3 Essential features to look for in a business format franchise

Standardization □ A unique selling point □ A high margin product □ Bulk purchasing □ Operational skills required by the franchisee □ Marketing the franchise □ Pilot operations □ Capital and skills required by the franchisor □ Personnel □ The operating manual □ The franchise contract □ Selection of suitable franchisees □ Training and continuing assistance given to franchisees □ Franchisor/franchisee relations □ Availability of suitable locations □ Support from a bank □ Membership of the British Franchise Association □ Checklist

No two franchise operations are identical and each one will have its own unique set of features, products, control systems etc. However, observation of established operations suggests a whole range of features which tend to recur time and time again in many of the more successful franchises.

The purpose of this chapter is to demonstrate that the idea that anything at all can be franchised with the minimum of effort is completely unfounded, and that in fact the franchisor will have to give very careful consideration to all aspects of his operation.

Standardization

Standardization is absolutely central to the whole concept of franchising. All franchise operations must demonstrate consistency in the following three areas:

   (a) in the products or services offered in each of their franchised outlets
   (b) in the way those products or services are offered
   (c) in the image presented to the public by each outlet.

The franchise chain as a whole will only be successful if the customer is confident that he will receive the same service in every single outlet in that chain. Failure to maintain consistent standards will quickly result in loss of customer goodwill. Therefore a particular franchise concept must be capable of exact duplication in every location.

Standard goods

In order to ensure standardization in all outlets, the franchisor must be able to maintain strict quality control. If one franchisee offers sub-standard products or services to the public, then the resulting loss of goodwill will affect all franchisees and, of course, the franchisor himself since the customer views all franchised outlets as being part of a national chain. Therefore if the customer is served with, say, a poor quality hamburger in a franchised fast food outlet, then his patronage will be lost not only to that particular outlet, but also to the franchise chain as a whole. For this reason many franchisees are contractually required to purchase all their supplies directly from the franchisor himself, or from suppliers nominated by the franchisor, in an attempt to ensure consistent standards of quality. A franchisee who purchases supplies from outside the franchise system risks lowering the quality of the final product and thereby hurting not only himself, but also the entire franchise chain.

Standard premises

Uniformity must extend not only to the actual products, but also to the environment in which they are sold. The franchisor must therefore ensure that all franchisees adhere strictly to the layout, colour scheme etc. stipulated for the premises. Similarly all the promotional material used by franchisees must be standard.

Only by ensuring that wherever possible standardization is introduced and adhered to can the franchisor hope to reproduce and maintain the corporate image on both a regional and a national (and even international) basis.

A unique selling point

In order for a business to be suitable for franchising it must have some sort of 'differential advantage'. In other words it must have some feature which is in some way distinctive or unique, giving it an advantage over its competitors. This might be a unique product, such as a secret ingredient in a fast food franchise, or some advantage in the service offered, e.g. speed of service. It is also important that this feature should be difficult for others to imitate – any competitive advantage will last only momentarily if competitors can quickly and easily incorporate the same idea into their own service. Where possible, special processes, methods, identifying marks etc., should be protected by patents or trade marks.

Market demand

As with any other business, the franchisor must try to identify a gap in the market which he can fill. The product or service which is to be offered should:

- be well designed
- have a highly marketable image
- have widespread appeal
- satisfy continuing demand rather than merely a temporary 'fad'.

Products which are subject to large seasonal sales fluctuations may be considered unsuitable for franchising, especially if the franchisees are contractually restricted from selling any products other than those of the franchisor. Franchising has been given exemption from European Community competition restrictions so that franchisors can in fact forbid franchisees from selling competing products. The imposition of such a contractual term is a further attempt by the franchisor to ensure standardization by closely controlling the product range sold by franchisees.

The franchisor must ensure that the franchisees will have access to a constant supply of materials and products used in the operation. He must therefore locate financially sound suppliers who will be able to provide the required quality and quantity of products over a long period. Frequent changes in the sources of supply will result in high 'search costs' for the franchisor and may cause fluctuating quality standards – a situation which clearly should be avoided if at all possible.

A high margin product

In order to survive, each outlet must be capable of generating a large enough profit both to provide the franchisee with an adequate return on his financial investment and personal effort, and to pay the franchisor a management services fee. Therefore the franchisee has to be able to earn a relatively high gross margin on sales, i.e. the difference between the selling price and the cost of products to the franchisee. Of course, the relative margin which can be earned will depend upon the type of business in which the franchisee operates. A franchisee in the grocery business will usually earn only a small margin on sales in percentage terms, because of the high degree of competition in the grocery trade, and must therefore achieve a high total turnover in order to generate enough total profit to provide an acceptable return for both himself and the franchisor.

Bulk purchasing

Gross margins are improved by the fact that franchisees will usually reap the benefit of centralized bulk purchasing by the franchisor who will pass on at least part of the quantity discount to the franchisees. Many franchisors should not add any mark-up on sales to franchisees, to ensure that the franchisee earns an adequate profit. If the franchisor passes on the whole of the benefit of quantity discounts to the franchisees, it means that franchisees pay significantly below wholesale price for their supplies. Franchisors may retain some of the benefit of bulk purchasing for themselves, partly to cover the administrative cost of purchasing and partly to increase their own profit. Even allowing for such a mark-up, the franchisee will usually end up paying a much lower price for his materials than he would if he were a totally independent non-franchised operator. Central purchasing by the franchisor also saves the franchisee a great deal of time and effort in purchasing since he only has to deal with one supplier – the franchisor.

Operational skills required by the franchisee

If a franchise is to be successful the franchisor must bear in mind that the skills involved in the business concept must be relatively simple to learn. If the concept relies heavily on a high degree of skill then it is unlikely to be suitable for franchising. It is clearly unrealistic to expect to be able to successfully franchise a business that would require the franchisee to spend a year learning the basic skills. The concept and techniques involved in the operation of the business must be simple enough so that the franchisee can learn them within a short space of time.

Marketing the franchise

If a franchisor is to stand any chance of being successful he must ensure that the franchise operation itself is carefully marketed. The franchisor has to decide whether he is going to undertake his own marketing campaign or whether he is going to employ the services of a 'franchise packager' who may provide a whole range of services from a feasibility study right through to a complete marketing plan. Franchise consultants are a common feature of the franchise industry in North America, and while there are not as many in the UK they do exist (see Appendix). Franchise consultants can be an invaluable source of information and advice for the prospective franchisor who is in the process of setting up his operation but does not yet have the necessary experience and knowledge. Established franchisors on the other hand will usually have their own 'in-house' expertise. Either way, the franchisor must consider exactly how he wishes to present his franchise to prospective franchisees, and he must be careful to avoid any bad publicity which may give him a lasting reputation as an unscrupulous, or 'fly-by-night' operator.

Pilot operations

All successful franchises have to be thoroughly tested in the marketplace before they are offered to prospective franchisees. Some franchisors wish to use the franchise technique in order to expand an existing business, and others (less commonly) develop a business from scratch specifically with franchising in mind. Either way, the business should be fully tested before being sold as a franchise in order to demonstrate that the proposed system will in fact work as a franchise. Therefore at least one, and preferably several franchisor-owned 'pilot outlets' should be set up. These should be operated using exactly the same processes and systems as those that the franchisees will be required to use in running their franchised outlets. The pilot schemes should be run for at least a year before the first franchise is sold if they are to provide a useful indicator of the potential success of the franchise, since it may take 12 months for any seasonal fluctuations or changes in the market to manifest themselves.

It is important to ensure that the success of the initial pilot operation was not just a fluke due to some unusually favourable set of circumstances which subsequent franchisees could not realistically expect to enjoy. Therefore several pilot operations should be tested in a cross-section of the markets in which franchises will be sold in order to take account of regional differences etc.

Similarly, differences in the ethnic origin or average income of residents in certain areas may mean that pilot outlets opened in these areas cannot be considered reliable guides to the potential of the franchise.

Purpose of pilot operations

Pilot operations are used as a means of testing every detail of the proposed franchise operation, including the operating manual (see below).

Revisions can be made to the franchise plan in the light of the experience gained through operation of pilot outlets before franchises are sold. It would be highly inadvisable to use the first franchisees as guinea-pigs, assuming that it would actually be possible to sell any franchises without having operated pilot schemes, as this will inevitably cause dissatisfaction and bad publicity if operations do not run to plan. This might eliminate the chance of ever being able to sell any more franchises.

Capital and skills required by the franchisor

It is vital that the franchisor does not underestimate the financial capital and skills that he will require in order to set up a franchise operation. The start-up costs involved in the franchise programme can be extremely high. The franchisor has to:

- establish the necessary organization
- meet all the professional fees
- compile the operating manual.

These will all require a substantial financial input. The total cost of establishing the franchise system may easily be in excess of £100 000 before a single franchise has been sold, and it may be three to five years before the operation breaks even. During this period the franchisees may require a lot of training and hand-holding. The franchisor must have adequate financial resources to keep the operation running through these initial years during which the management services fees received from franchisees may be very low yet demands made upon the franchisor are high. The capital problem is compounded further if the franchisor supplies the materials needed by the franchisees as he will have to finance a substantial investment in stocks.

Personnel

The franchisor also has to ensure that he has adequate human resources during the initial years. He may need to recruit people specially to train the franchisees, and he will have to hire the necessary administrative staff. If he himself intends to concentrate on recruiting franchisees he will have to hire additional managerial talent to run the company-owned outlets effectively while he devotes his effort to selling the franchise. It is particularly important that the company-owned outlets are not ignored since they will probably have to provide the essential cash-flow for the franchisor during the early years.

The franchisor must also recognize the fact that he is no longer primarily in the business of, say, selling hamburgers – he is now in the business of setting franchisees up in business to sell hamburgers. This requires different skills from those that he has needed in the past. Strong skills are essential in the areas of:

- finance
- administration
- marketing.

The operating manual

The operating manual is a detailed document containing all the rules governing the overall management procedures and day-to-day running of the franchise. The franchise contract should clearly stipulate that the franchisee is obliged to follow the instructions laid down in the operating manual. This helps to ensure standardization of the services offered by all franchisees, thereby protecting the uniform image of the franchise system.

The operating manual should be drawn up as soon as possible after the decision has been made to offer franchises. Not only does this allow any amendments to be made in the light of experience gained through operating the pilot outlets, but it should also help to make the franchisor aware in advance of all the possible problems which may arise. A carefully constructed operating manual may well make the difference between success and failure for the franchise operation, as the 'rules of the game' are clearly laid out before the franchisee commences trading. All successful franchise operations have a highly comprehensive operating manual, often stretching to several hundred pages.

The franchise contract

All the terms of the franchise should be clearly stated in the contract in order to avoid arguments between the franchisee and franchisor over ambiguities at a later stage. The franchisor should resist the temptation to negotiate special deals with individual franchisees. This inflexible approach might cost the franchisor a few potential franchisees but it ensures that all franchisees get exactly the same deal from the franchisor. If one franchisee finds out from another that he has not been given quite as good a deal as some other franchisees this may lead to dissatisfaction, resentment and mistrust on the franchisee's part.

The contract should include details of:

- the initial fee and management services fee to be paid by the franchisee
- the franchisor's obligations regarding continuing assistance
- whether the franchisee can only sell products approved of by the franchisor or not
- whether the franchisee has been granted an exclusive territory
- the duration of the contract
- the circumstances under which it can be terminated by either party
- who pays for promotion.

(See Chapter 10 for a fuller discussion of the franchise contract.)

The contract is one of the most important ingredients in any successful franchise operation. It must adequately protect the intellectual property of the franchisor without being unfair to the franchisee, and must leave no ambiguities. The contract, combined with the operating manual should cover every single aspect of the operation of the franchise.

Selection of suitable franchisees

Having fully planned the franchise operation, run the pilot outlets for a year or more, and having drawn up the operating manual and the franchise contract, the franchisor now has to find potential franchisees. It is vital that the franchisor selects suitable candidates, particularly in the early days of the franchise operation. Initially the franchisor may be tempted to accept the first applicants who show interest in order to secure quickly the sale of the first franchises and get the operation off the ground. However, a hasty decision may result in the acceptance of franchisees who later turn out to be unsuitable, and the success of the entire franchise system may consequently be jeopardized. It may then be very difficult to convince subsequent applicants that earlier failures were due to the inadequacies of the franchisees rather than of the operation itself.

Who makes a good franchisee?

- The franchisee does not normally require extensive experience in the particular business field concerned since the franchisor will provide comprehensive training. In fact many franchisors refuse to accept applicants who have had previous experience in that field of operation since it is felt that such candidates might be too set in their ways and will be unwilling to operate the business according to the methods stipulated by the franchisor. For example, many printing franchise operations refuse to accept as franchisees people who have previously worked in the printing industry. Most franchisors insist that the franchisees should be involved in the day-to-day running of the franchise, and are unwilling to accept absentee owners.

- Franchisors look for franchisees who not only have the necessary capital, but who also display the required business acumen and basic managerial skills. There is, however, an increased danger with franchisees who have extensive managerial experience that they will begin to question the control placed upon them.

- Someone who is fiercely independent is unlikely to make a suitable franchisee as he will soon begin to resent the continuing controls imposed upon him by the franchisor. Franchisors might, therefore, be advised to look for some entrepreneurial qualities in franchisees but should avoid people who clearly see themselves as 'originators' rather than 'followers'.

- A franchisee will usually find himself working harder than he has ever done in the past (especially if he has no previous experience of self-employment), and may have to work for extended periods without a day off. He will therefore need to be physically fit and for this reason some franchisors put an upper age limit on people they will consider for franchises. The franchisee must also be sure of the support of his family who will almost inevitably become involved in the franchise – even if this means nothing more than answering the telephone!

- The franchisee must be willing to provide a significant amount of the capital needed for the franchise out of his personal resources. This requirement ensures that the franchisee is suitably motivated to make the business work.

Beyond these guidelines it is very difficult to define the 'ideal' franchisee. Many franchisors develop a profile of the sort of person they are looking for. However, such a profile can be used only as an initial screening device. At the end of the day, selecting a franchisee will inevitably be largely a process of intuition.

Training and continuing assistance given to franchisees

One of the most attractive aspects of franchising from the franchisee's point of view is that he requires much less previous experience than he would if he were opening his own wholly independent non-franchised business. Franchisors provide extensive training in all aspects of the running of the business, including the day-to-day operational skills and the management techniques that are required. The training will usually include elements of both 'classroom' teaching, and actual experience working in an existing outlet, either franchised or franchisor-owned. It is in the interests of both parties that this training should be as comprehensive as possible. A highly trained franchisee is likely to get his business off the ground more rapidly, and extensive training in all the operating methods leaves less scope for the franchisee to develop his own 'bad habits' or non-standard techniques. In other words, this is an integral part of the standardization and control process. Furthermore, a fully trained franchisee is likely to need less initial hand-holding, thus leaving the franchisor free to concentrate on the overall strategic management of the operation and selling franchises.

Continuing assistance

In addition to the initial training, the franchisee will also need continuing assistance and advice from the franchisor. Once again, it is in their mutual interests that the franchisor ensures that any problems that arise are dealt with promptly and effectively. If problems are not sorted out expediently then the franchisee will soon begin to resent having to pay the franchisor a continuing management services fee on turnover, and will quickly become dissatisfied. This may be reflected in the service offered to the public, which, as already stated, harms all participants in the franchise chain. Therefore all successful franchise chains have effective methods of dealing with franchisee problems, and adopt a sympathetic and under-standing approach to franchisees when they encounter difficulties. In order for this approach to work well, the franchisor has to develop an effective two-way communications system between the franchisee and himself. The franchisee should feel confident that he can contact head office at any time. On the other hand, while the franchisor will seek to centralize control over many aspects of the operation, he will not wish to be involved in every aspect of the day-to-day running of each outlet. He must therefore be willing to delegate sufficient authority to the franchisees in order to allow them to be able to take appropriate decisions at 'branch level' (providing that they do not break any of the rules laid down in the operating manual).

Franchisor/franchisee relations

A successful franchise relationship relies heavily on mutual trust between the two parties. The franchisor has to trust the franchisee to make appropriate operating decisions concerning the daily operation of his outlet, and similarly the franchisee has to feel confident that assistance is available from the franchisor should it be needed. The relationship will turn sour as soon as either party begins to mistrust the other. This is one of the reasons why the operating manual and the franchise contract should be as comprehensive as possible so that both parties know from the outset exactly what their rights and obligations are.

Availability of suitable locations

As in most types of retailing, the key to successful franchising is the availability of suitable locations. The franchisor should identify exactly what level of pedestrian traffic, access, nearby parking etc. is required for an outlet to be considered 'suitable'. Clearly this will depend upon the type of business in which the franchise operates. A business that relies mainly on impulse purchases will need a location with a much higher traffic flow than will be required by a highly specialized outlet to which customers make planned visits (e.g. a drain clearance franchise).

The rapid growth in the popularity of shopping malls has been a great boon to franchising. Many franchises are purposely designed so that they require premises with only a relatively small floor area in order that the total rental cost will be reasonably low even in prime locations where the charge per square foot is high. Franchisees can therefore afford to lease space in the expensive, high traffic malls. Suitable premises in the UK are becoming increasingly scarce, and franchisors should take account of this fact when designing their outlets. They must determine the current and future availability of suitable sites within a price range that the franchisees will be able to afford.

Many franchisors reserve the right to make the final decision in the selection of a site for a new franchise. A proportion of the initial fee paid by the franchisee is often used to finance a complete market survey in order to establish the viability of the proposed location. The franchisor will often impose fairly detailed stipulations of the features which he considers necessary in a site. Site selection is one of the most important elements not only in franchising but in any successful retail operation.

In some cases the franchisor may own many of the premises from which franchisees operate. This not only increases the franchisor's revenue (through rent collected from the franchisee), but it also makes it easier for the franchisee to find suitable sites. Alternatively, the franchisor will sometimes lease the premises from a landlord who is unwilling to accept the franchisee as a lessee for fear that he might default on the rent payments. The franchisor will therefore guarantee the rent payments, and will sub-lease the property to the franchisee.

Support from a bank

While it is not essential for the franchisor to have arranged a special financing package for franchisees with a bank, the franchisor should, at the very least, have acquainted the clearing banks with full details of the operation.

Membership of the British Franchise Association

Once again this is by no means absolutely essential for a successful franchise, but prospective franchisees are almost bound to ask whether the franchisor is a member of the BFA, and if he is not, why not. Membership of the BFA should increase the credibility of the franchisor since the Association requires its members to meet a stringent set of qualifying conditions, and to adhere to a code of ethics (see Chapter 8). Membership is therefore likely to be an extremely useful asset in recruiting franchisees.

Checklist

To have a chance of being successful, the business to be franchised *must*:

● be capable of standardization
● have a unique selling point
● have a relatively high profit margin
● be simple for the franchisees to operate.

To set up the franchise the franchisor will have to:

● market the franchise
● set up at least one pilot operation.
● have sufficient capital and skills to support the network
● draw up a comprehensive operating manual
● draw up a detailed contract
● select suitable franchisees
● train the franchisees and give them continuing assistance when they are operating their outlets
● ensure good franchisor/franchisee relations
● find suitable locations for the franchise outlets.
● provide details to clearing banks
● consider merits of BFA membership.

4 The advantages and disadvantages of franchising for the franchisee

The advantages for the franchisee □ The disadvantages for the franchisee

The advantages for the franchisee

Franchising offers the franchisee many advantages in comparison with setting up a totally independent business – some of the most important benefits include the following.

Established products

The franchisee starts in business with the use of an established trade name and corporate image, a proven product or service, and the benefit of the goodwill that has been built up by the franchisor. He therefore starts from a much more favourable position than someone who is setting up a totally independent business without any existing goodwill etc. A franchisee will find entry into the market much easier than he would if he were to 'go it alone'.

Previous experience unnecessary

The franchisee does not usually require any previous experience of self-employment or of the particular industry in which he will be operating, since he will receive full training and continuing managerial assistance from the franchisor. The franchise system is therefore an ideal route into self-employment for an individual who has little or no relevant experience, as opposed to starting a totally independent enterprise which will usually require some experience or knowledge in the proposed field of business. In other words, even if a person lacks the requisite 'human capital' (i.e. personal skills) to start their own independent business they may well be capable of operating a franchise.

Improved success rate

Because the franchisee enjoys the benefit of the use of an established trade mark, and the initial and ongoing managerial assistance that is provided by the franchisor, his chances of success are significantly greater than would be the case if he were to start his own independent business. Statistics on business failure rates vary greatly (depending upon exactly how 'failure' is defined), but it has often been suggested that while 90 per cent of new businesses fail within the first five years of start-up, the corresponding figure for franchisees is less than 10 per cent.

Raising finance

As a result of the reduced risk of failure, the franchisee should find that it is far easier to raise finance (usually at lower interest rates) for a franchised outlet than would be the case for an independent start-up. Furthermore, the franchisor will usually assist the franchisee in finding sources of finance and in many cases will have arranged a special finance package with one of the major clearing banks. These packages are tailor-made for the franchisee's needs and the terms offered are usually very favourable. Thus the relative ease with which franchisees can attract finance is one of the major benefits of the franchise system.

Less competition

The franchisee will usually enjoy some sort of protection against competition from other franchisees in the same franchise network. Contractual terms which grant exclusive territorial rights to franchisees must be worded very carefully otherwise they are likely to be in breach of the Restrictive Trade Practices Act 1976. However, recent European Commission regulations allow the practice of restricting franchisees to specific geographical territories. This prevents franchisees in the same franchise chain from 'poaching' each other's business.

Franchisor assistance

The franchisor will provide assistance in locating a suitable site for the franchisee, selection of equipment, appropriate stock levels etc.

Lower start-up costs

Start-up costs are often lower for a franchise than for a similar independent business. The initial expenses relating to the launch of the franchisee's outlet are also usually deployed more effectively since the franchisor has the benefit of significant experience in setting up and launching new outlets.

Lower operating costs

The franchisee's operating costs may also be lower as a result of bulk central purchasing by the franchisor, economies of scale in advertising and promotion, staff training programmes organized by the franchisor, etc.

Advertising

The franchisee will benefit from both regional and national advertising which is undertaken by the franchisor on a scale which would be completely beyond the resources of the independent businessman.

No development costs

4

The franchisor will constantly be seeking ways to improve his system. The franchisee will benefit from any such developments without having to undertake expensive and time-consuming research and experimentation.

Learn from others

The franchisee will usually have many opportunities to discuss particular problems, different operating methods, etc. with his fellow franchisees in the network on both a formal and an informal basis. He is therefore able to share his problems and learn from the experience of other franchisees.

Idea and know-how provided

Many people have a desire to run their own small business rather than be an employee, but either lack an initial idea of exactly what they would like to do, or do not know how to go about setting up their own business. Franchising provides an ideal opportunity for these people, especially since such a large range of businesses is now available as franchises.

The disadvantages for the franchisee

Franchisor controls

One of the major disadvantages of the franchise system is that although the franchisee is a legally independent businessman, the franchisor will exert a fairly high degree of control over the franchisee and his operation. Many franchisees find this control extremely frustrating, particularly once they have been operating for some time and possibly feel that they no longer need the continuing assistance of the franchisor. (This control is, however, essential in ensuring uniformity and standardization in all outlets in order to maintain the goodwill enjoyed by all participants in the franchise.)

Lack of adaptability

In addition to the psychological disadvantage of this continuing control, the franchisee's business may suffer to some degree because he may be prevented from making necessary adaptations to his operation in response to changes in specific local tastes, conditions etc.

Collective bad publicity

Any bad publicity surrounding the franchisor is likely to have a detrimental knock-on effect on the franchisee's business. Similarly, the franchisee is likely to suffer if the actions of any other franchisee in the network cause any loss of goodwill or bad publicity. The franchisee must therefore accept that while he enjoys the benefits of being seen as part of a larger franchise chain with a national reputation etc., this association can just as easily have detrimental effects.

Management service fee

The franchisee has to pay some form of continuing fee to the franchisor. He may come to resent having to make these ongoing payments and might feel that the franchisor is doing little to justify them, particularly once his outlet is well established and the franchisor has a much less apparent involvement in his operation.

Expectations unfulfilled

The franchise may fail to meet the franchisee's expectations (in terms of both profit and psychological satisfaction). This situation may arise if the franchisor 'over-sold' the operation (or even went so far as to totally mislead the franchisee). The franchisee will have paid some amount for use of the franchisor's trade marks, the benefit of his goodwill, etc. yet these may turn out to be effectively worthless. (This problem is much less likely to arise if the franchisee takes independent professional financial and legal advice before purchasing a franchise.)

Restrictions on termination

The franchisee has a contractual obligation to continue to operate his outlet and the circumstances under which he can terminate the agreement may be fairly restrictive. Furthermore, under the terms of the franchise contract, he may not necessarily be allowed to sell his business to whomsoever he likes – the franchisor will normally reserve the right to vet potential purchasers in order to ensure that they are acceptable to him as franchisees.

The relative importance of each of these advantages and disadvantages will vary between different franchise operations and between different franchisees. In addition to these more common considerations each individual franchise opportunity will have its own specific problems and benefits. Clearly it is important for any potential franchisee to bear this in mind when considering a specific franchise operation.

5 The advantages and disadvantages of franchising for the franchisor

The advantages for the franchisor □ The disadvantages for the franchisor □ Trust

There are two situations in which the franchising system can be employed:

(a) where a business concept is developed with franchising specifically in mind as a means of generating income for the originator;

(b) where a company is seeking a means of achieving wider distribution for its products or expansion for its service. In this case franchising can be used as an alternative method of expansion to setting up company-owned outlets.

In the first case franchising is an end in itself, whereas in the second it is merely a means to an end. Naturally the franchising alternative offers both advantages and disadvantages for the franchisor. The major arguments both for and against opening franchised outlets are described below:

The advantages for the franchisor

Rapid expansion

The franchisor can achieve extremely rapid expansion of his distribution network without having to borrow substantial funds or raise additional equity finance, since the franchisees own their outlets and supply the necessary capital. Thus he can develop an extensive national market presence much more quickly, and using less of his own capital than would be the case if he were to open company-owned outlets instead. Consequently, many franchisors have used the franchising system in order to secure a large market share much more rapidly than they otherwise could possibly have hoped to achieve. From a strategic point of view this is extremely important because early entry into a market and a large market share is usually associated with greater profitability and increased resilience to competitive forces.

Motivation of franchisees

Because franchisees actually own their outlets and are required to make a substantial financial investment in their operation, they will usually be much more highly motivated than hired managers to maximize sales and reduce costs in order to increase profits. (This motivation is often referred to as the 'franchising ethic'.) Since franchisees generally achieve higher sales levels than hired managers, the franchisor will usually find that he can achieve a larger market share by franchising outlets than he could by opening the same number of company-owned units. Furthermore, franchised outlets will often be more profitable for the franchisor than company-owned units.

Delegation of authority

The franchisor is freed from having to deal with many of the day-to-day management problems of individual outlets. He delegates authority and control to the franchisees, and wherever possible avoids interfering in their daily operation. The franchisor therefore requires only a relatively small head office staff and consequently his overheads and personnel problems are minimized.

Increased competitiveness

The franchisor is better able to compete on equal terms with larger rival companies. He can reap the benefits of greater negotiating strength with suppliers because he is buying in bulk on behalf of many franchisees and is therefore in a position to demand substantial quantity discounts, better payment terms, etc.

Stability of personnel

Since franchisees own their outlets they are likely to operate those outlets for a much longer period of time than hired managers would. A hired manager constantly seeks promotion either within the organization or by moving to another company in order to further his long-term career prospects. The long-term prospects for the franchisee, however, lie in the success of his individual outlet. Naturally therefore, he will tend to maintain ownership and control of his outlet for a relatively long period of time. It is a much greater step for a franchisee to sell his outlet in order to find some other business venture (or go back to employee status) than it is for a hired manager to change his job. Thus the franchisor benefits from a much more stable distribution network and spends less time (and money) training new managers. Apart from the desirability of a stable network from an organizational and administrative point of view, it also leads to greater efficiency as it will take some time for new managers to ride down the learning curve, i.e. they will not achieve full efficiency until they have been in control of an outlet for some time since they have to 'learn the ropes' – even if a manager has gained extensive experience in one outlet, if he is subsequently moved to another location he will not be totally familiar with all the systems used in the new unit, the staff, the local trading conditions etc. Therefore, frequent changes in managerial personnel imply less than maximum efficiency.

One of the major problems in retailing is finding the right store manager and staff and then paying them a large enough salary to retain them once they have been trained. Under the franchising system, however, the problem of turnover of key personnel is radically reduced.

Local knowledge

Franchisees will have a much better knowledge of the local market and its peculiarities than hired managers appointed by head office. Thus franchising is likely to result in better service on a localized basis and consequently greater turnover and profit.

Increased control

A company that wishes to open an outlet in a location that is either geographically isolated, or is some distance from head office, will often find that franchising is the best means of overcoming many of the problems of controlling such a remote outlet. (This is one of the major reasons why franchising has become a popular means of expansion in North America, since it is such a vast continent.) Franchising is an excellent means of operating a chain consisting of a large number of geographically dispersed outlets where the quality of personnel is crucial to the success of the enterprise as a whole. The franchisees' motivation should ensure that the customer-retailer relationship is maintained to the highest standard without the need for constant head office supervision and control.

Viable marginal outlets

A franchised outlet may be viable in a 'marginal' location where a company-owned outlet would be uneconomic because the manager's salary would eliminate any profit. In this situation the franchisee is effectively buying himself the right to a manager's job. The increased motivation of the franchisee (i.e. the franchising ethic, described earlier) may be sufficient to increase turnover and reduce costs to a level adequate enough both to provide the franchisee with an income and also to be able to pay a management services fee to the franchisor. The franchisor therefore benefits from income which he would not otherwise have, and at the same time benefits from an increased market presence.

Divergent economies of scale

Some industries are characterized by 'divergent' economies of scale. In other words the optimum scale of operation differs substantially at different points in the production and sales processes. For example, in the motor industry, cars must be manufactured on an extremely large scale using mass production techniques in order to achieve the necessary economies of scale. The retailing of the finished product on the other hand is best achieved on a much smaller scale using a large number of relatively small localized outlets. For many customers a car is the second most expensive item they will ever buy (after their house!) and they therefore demand a standard of service from the distributor that is difficult to achieve using the sort of huge organisational structure that is necessary for the efficient manaufacture of the product. Similarly, a fast food chain can be promoted most effectively on a national scale, but actually serving customers is best carried out using a decentralized organization and locally delegated control.

Franchising is probably one of the best ways of overcoming the problems associated with divergent economies of scale as it allows the manufacturing, advertising, central management, administration etc. to be carried out on a large centralized basis by the franchisor, thereby reaping the economies of large scale, while allowing the retailing to be carried out on a much smaller scale on a local basis by franchisees. Thus tasks are divided between the franchisor and the franchisee in a way that in each case minimizes the average cost of performing the tasks involved.

The disadvantages for the franchisor

Franchisees, not employees

Most of the major disadvantages of franchising from the franchisor's point of view stem from the fact that, unlike a hired manager, the franchisee is not an employee and therefore cannot simply be ordered to follow instructions. Consequently, one of the major problems faced by the franchisor is the difficulty of ensuring that all franchisees adhere to standard operating methods in order to achieve uniformity in all outlets. This is a problem that is in no way exclusive to franchising – it arises with hired managers in company-owned outlets – but the franchisor does not exert the same direct control over a franchisee as he does over an employee. The franchisor may therefore have great problems in persuading franchisees to follow recommended practices on a day-to-day basis, and inevitably there may be some lack of standardization between different franchised outlets.

Differing objectives

The objectives of the franchisees regarding profit (both long and short-term), turnover, corporate image, etc, may not coincide with those of the franchisor. This is likely to lead rapidly to disputes and a lack of co-operation between the two parties. Once again, because of the franchisor's lack of absolute control over the franchisee, there may be little he can do to rectify such a situation.

Resentment of control

Whilst the franchisee may initially be very content in his new business venture, he may begin to resent the continuing control that the franchisor exerts over his activities. This can lead to a breakdown in the all-important relationship between the two parties and may eventually result in sub-standard service in the outlets concerned. (This problem is more fully discussed in Chapter 9.)

Unsuitable franchisees

The franchise contract will only allow the franchisor to terminate the agreement under certain circumstances. Therefore, if he initially selects franchisees who subsequently turn out to be inappropriate, for whatever reason, his only alternative may be to offer to buy back their outlets from them at an inflated price. Obviously the franchisor is not able to 'sack' a franchisee or move him to a different post in the way that he could with a hired manager.

Profitability

In some cases the franchisor may find that franchised outlets are less profitable than company-owned operations.

Policing franchisees

The franchisor has the problem of somehow 'policing' the franchisees in order to ensure that they are not under-declaring sales and thereby avoiding the payment of management services fees.

Rival operations

The franchisor has to accept that once the franchisee is fully conversant with the franchisor's operating system he may sell his franchise and set up a similar operation of his own in direct competition with the franchisor. Thus he will have the advantage of a detailed knowledge of the franchisor's know-how, management systems, operating techniques, etc. Many franchise contracts include a clause which states that the franchisee is forbidden from operating a similar business within a given territory for a given length of time after the termination of the agreement.

As with the advantages and disadvantages to the franchisee, the relative importance of each of the above points will differ from one franchise operation to the next, and each franchisor will experience other additional benefits and problems unique to his own specific circumstances.

5

Trust

Most of the advantages and disadvantages described in this and the previous chapter highlight the fact that the franchise relationship is largely based on mutual trust and dependence. It is extremely important that both the franchisor and the franchisee realize, before entering into a franchise agreement, that their respective fortunes are inextricably linked. It is this fact which gives rise to many of the advantages and disadvantages from both points of view.

6 The cost of purchasing a franchise

The initial franchise fee □ Fees for continuing services provided by the franchisor □ Management services fee on turnover □ A mark-up on materials purchased from the franchisor □ Advantages and disadvantages of fees and mark-up □ Fixed and minimum franchise fees □ Charges for equipment purchased through the franchisor □ Leasing charges paid for premises/equipment □ Contributions made to an advertising fund □ Checklist

In buying a franchise the franchisee will incur all the normal expenses that are involved in starting any business. These include the cost of construction, leases, equipment, fixtures and fittings, stock, working capital, etc. However, in addition to these usual costs a franchisee will incur some expenses over and above those faced by a wholly independent businessman. Many of the various costs associated with the purchase of a franchise will be paid directly to the franchisor. Some of the more important expenses which the franchisee may be obliged to pay to the franchisor include:

● An initial (or 'front-end') franchise fee.
● Continuing fees in consideration for ongoing services provided by the franchisor.
● Charges for equipment purchased through the franchisor.
● Leasing charges for premises and equipment.
● Contributions to an advertising fund.

The initial franchise fee

In virtually all cases the franchisee will be required to pay an initial (or 'front-end') fee to the franchisor. In theory this fee is supposed to cover the costs incurred by the franchisor in setting up a new outlet, including the following items:

● The cost of developing the franchise manual

- Design costs
- The cost of developing the accounting system
- The cost of site selection
- The cost of the initial training provided by the franchisor
- The cost of marketing the franchise system
- The cost of initial advertising and promotion for the launch of the franchisee's individual outlet
- Professional fees and legal costs
- Initial store supervision by the franchisor
- Travel and accommodation
- The franchisor's own time

The initial fee may also include an amount in consideration for the right to use the franchisor's intellectual property (i.e. his trade marks, corporate image, etc.).

The level of the initial fee

In order to determine the appropriate level at which to set the initial franchise fee the franchisor must first estimate all the costs that he will incur in developing the franchise network. For example, the cost of setting up a service industry franchise with a small regional network might be somewhere in the region of £50000, whereas the cost for a national network might be nearer £200000, not including the cost of pilot operations. The franchisor will seek to recover this total cost over a reasonable number of franchised outlets so he must therefore also estimate how many franchises he can reasonably expect to sell. Having made these two estimates the franchisor then at least has a starting point from which he can begin to calculate what he would consider to be an appropriate initial fee.

However, the story does not end there – there are additional factors which must be taken into consideration before determining the actual level of the initial fee that should be charged. There is a widely-held view in the British franchising industry that it is unethical for the initial fee to cover very much more than the cost of setting the franchisee up in business, and that front-end fees should not be a source of profit for the franchisor. This is the viewpoint adopted by the British Franchise Association, who suggest that the franchisor's earnings should be generated from continuing management services fees so that they are motivated to ensure that the operation continues to run successfully, and that the initial franchise fee should only be sufficient to cover the costs incurred by the franchisor in starting the franchisee up in business. It is argued that a high initial fee may place an excessive financial burden on the franchisee, and is open to exploitation by fraudulent operators seeking to make their profits purely from selling outlets and who may subsequently fail to provide the franchisee with adequate support once his outlet is in operation.

As a general guide the front-end fee should represent about 10 per cent of the total initial investment required of the franchisee. It is likely to be proportionately more, however, with a low cost franchise than with one of higher cost.

Resistance towards high initial franchise fees developed largely as a result of the emergence of pyramid selling in the 1960s. Pyramid selling is a highly dubious system involving the sale of the right to distribute a given product in return for an initial fee. However, the main objective of the system is not to achieve a distribution network for the product, but simply to recruit as many distributors as possible, thereby collecting large revenues in the form of initial fees. Existing distributors are given what appear to be very attractive financial incentives to recruit further distributors. Of course the main beneficiaries of the scheme are the fraudulent originators. During the pyramid selling era the image of franchising suffered as the public erroneously confused franchising with the pyramid selling technique. Pyramid sellers usually adopted a hard-sell approach and charged high joining fees. Thus resistance developed to any system (including franchise operations) that involved a high front-end fee. Even though the pyramid selling era has long since passed and legislation has been introduced in an attempt to eliminate such fraudulent activities, the resistance to substantial initial fees has remained.

Advantages and disadvantages of high initial fees

Many UK franchisors may find that the level of fee that they are able to charge will be inadequate even to cover the direct costs of establishing a unit. Consequently they might have to recover these costs in the form of higher continuing fees than they would otherwise have charged.

One obvious advantage to the franchisor of minimizing the initial fee is of course that this should result in increased demand for franchises.

One of the major disadvantages of restricting the level of the initial franchise fee from the franchisor's point of view is that in the early months of starting the system he will experience a net cash outflow because the front-end fees are likely to be insufficient to cover the costs incurred in setting up individual outlets. Furthermore, it may take some time before outlets reach their full sales potential and therefore the income from continuing fees, which are usually based on turnover, will also be limited in the early days of the operation. The franchisor must therefore ensure that he has sufficient working capital to finance his operation during its early months. The franchisor-owned pilot outlets are very often used to provide the necessary cash-flow during the initial period until the revenues from franchisees start to flow.

Payment of the fee

The initial fee is usually paid as a single lump sum at the time at which the franchise contract is signed. If the contract is renewed after expiration of the initial term, the franchisee should not be required to pay a further full 'initial' fee since the franchisor does not have to incur the training costs, etc. again. A requirement to pay a second fee might destroy some of the goodwill built up between the two parties during the initial period.

Fees for continuing services provided by the franchisor

The franchisee will be required to pay some form of continuing fee to the franchisor in addition to the initial fee. This continuing fee is intended to reward the franchisor for the continuing management advice and assistance that he provides. The continuing fee is usually cited as being the main source of income for the franchisor and makes the greatest contribution towards his central overheads. It can be paid in one of three ways:

- A percentage on turnover (also known as a 'management services fee').
- A mark-up on materials purchased from the franchisor.
- A regular fixed amount per outlet.

Management services fee on turnover

A management services fee (i.e. a fixed percentage of turnover) is the most common form of continuing fee paid by franchisees. (Approximately 85 per cent of UK franchisors collect services fees from their franchisees.) In a minority of cases there may be at least some minimum charge payable by the franchisee regardless of the level of turnover that he achieves. In practice this system is generally frowned upon and is rarely employed. From a motivational point of view it is important that all franchisees are initially offered the same deal. The franchisor must therefore determine the appropriate services fee to charge his franchisees before he actually sells the first franchise. In order to do this he must forecast the sales and results which might be achieved in a 'typical' outlet in a 'typical' location.

His forecasts should be based on the results achieved in the pilot outlets, after making adjustments for the following items in order to maintain comparability:

- management salaries,
- extraordinary market conditions (e.g. weather/location, etc.),
- financing costs (which should be eliminated since they will vary greatly from one outlet to the next),
- perks such as company cars.

'Expected value' of turnover

One line of approach might be as follows:

The franchisor would make three forecasts of the turnover that might be achieved – a pessimistic forecast, a 'most likely' forecast, and an optimistic forecast. For each of these three turnover forecasts the probability of each one actually arising would also be estimated. Each of the three turnover forecasts would then be multiplied by its corresponding probability, and the resulting three figures would be added together to arrive at the 'expected value' of turnover. This figure can then be used as a basis for determining the services fee percentage which the franchisor must charge in order to cover his costs and leave himself with an acceptable profit. As a general guide the services fee percentage should be set at a level that will allow the franchisee to earn a return of, say, 20 per cent on his investment.

Setting the level of management services fee

The fee level will to a great extent be determined by the nature of the business concerned. For example, grocery stores tend to operate on very low margins but achieve a high turnover. The services fee payable by a franchisee operating in this area should therefore also be low. A service business on the other hand will usually have a lower turnover but much higher margins and lower overheads. Hence the franchise services fee will be larger. Competition between franchisors will also have an effect on the services fees charged within a given industry. From the franchisee's point of view the best method of determining whether or not the services fees charged by a particular franchisor are fair is simply to make comparisons with the services fees charged by other franchisors operating within the same field (NB when making comparisons between different operations, the services fees figure cannot be considered in isolation – the size of the initial fees charged in each case, the services provided by each franchisor, etc. must also be taken into account).

Once again there is a widely quoted rule of thumb that regardless of the above considerations, the services fees charged by a franchisor in respect of management services should not exceed about 10 per cent of turnover. Nonetheless, the fee should not be too low since the franchisor may then be unable to collect sufficient income in order to be able to provide the ongoing services promised in the franchise agreement. It is unwise to suggest any hard and fast rules as to what level of services fee should be paid, but it has been suggested that on average a UK franchisee should expect to pay to the franchisor somewhere between 20 per cent and 33 per cent of his annual trading profit, i.e. profit before deduction of various arbitrary items such as his own remuneration, or items highly specific to his individual circumstances such as interest and taxation.

A further somewhat peripheral benefit of a services fees system from the franchisor's point of view is that he will then be justified in requiring the franchisee to provide a weekly sales analysis, and will therefore have an accurate and up-to-date source of information on franchisee performance.

A mark-up on materials purchased from the franchisor

As an alternative to the services fee on turnover, the franchisee may be required to purchase some or all of his materials and supplies either direct from the franchisor himself, or from nominated suppliers. Under this system the franchisor generates his income by adding a mark-up to the goods purchased by the franchisee, or alternatively by receiving a commission from the nominated suppliers. The appropriate level of such a mark-up might be calculated in a similar way as for a services fee.

Advantages and disadvantages of fees and mark-up

Both the management services fee and mark-up methods have their own particular advantages and problems.

The managment services fee method

There are two main problems associated with the services fee method. First of all the franchisor has the problem of trying to ensure that the franchisee is actually declaring all of his turnover to the franchisor. The temptation for the franchisee is to under-declare his turnover and thereby reduce the services fee payments that he has to make. The mark-up method avoids this problem since the franchisor's margin is included in the price of all materials purchased by the franchisee.

Methods of checking franchisees' turnover. If a services fee system is used, the problem of 'policing' the franchisees in order to ensure that the franchisor knows exactly what level of turnover the franchisee is actually achieving can be largely overcome through the implementation of appropriate control systems. Consider the example of a fast food franchise.

All franchisees might be given an electronic till linked directly to the franchisor's head office. Thus all sales records would automatically be available to the franchisor.

The franchisees may be obliged to order some or all of their ingredients through the franchisor who will aggregate all the orders from all the franchisees and then place bulk orders with suppliers. The ingredients are then delivered direct from the suppliers to the franchisees at cost. Under this sort of system all orders for supplies are channelled through the franchisor, who consequently knows exactly what quantities of ingredients have been purchased by each franchisee. He can use this information to estimate with a high degree of accuracy the level of turnover that each franchisee should be declaring. A significant deviation of declared sales from expected sales may be the first signal that a franchisee is under-declaring his turnover in order to reduce the services fee payments made to the franchisor.

Franchisees could of course try to deceive the franchisor by purchasing ingredients independently so that they could avoid part of their service payments. However, the discounts that are usually secured through centralized bulk purchasing are often sufficient to outweigh any savings that franchisees might make by avoiding services fee payments.

The franchisor might even maintain a record of the amount of packaging supplied to each franchisee. It is very difficult for a franchisee to justify declared sales of only 10000 units if he has used 20000 bags!

Thus the problem of under-declaration of sales by franchisees who are attempting to avoid services fees payments can, to a large extent, be overcome if the franchisor implements suitable control systems.

Monthly services fee payments. A second problem associated with services fee payments is that the franchisee has to write a substantial cheque for the franchisor at the end of each month. From a psychological point of view this is likely to be a much more 'painful' way of paying the continuing fee than a mark-up which is included in the purchase price of materials. Franchisees may eventually come to resent having to continue to make this monthly payment, particularly once their outlets are fully established and they begin to feel that the franchisor is playing a decreasing role in their continued success. In order to overcome this problem the franchisor must continually (but subtly) emphasize the importance of the role that he plays in the franchisee's operation. In some cases a franchisor may try to avoid the problem through the use of a reducing payment system whereby the services fee payable by franchisees decreases in one or more incremental stages over time. (In practice this approach is rarely adopted.)

The mark-up method

The need for 'policing' is not totally eliminated simply by charging a mark-up rather than a services fee on turnover. The franchisees may be tempted to buy cheaper supplies from sources other than the franchisor and thereby avoid paying the mark-up, despite the fact that the contract might specifically forbid external purchasing. This would not only reduce the franchisor's income, but it might also result in the use of non-standard or inferior products. This would inevitably damage the customer goodwill enjoyed by the chain.

The major problem associated with the use of a mark-up is that the franchisee may feel that he is being exploited by the franchisor, especially if the franchisor does not disclose to the franchisees exactly what mark-up is applied to purchases. Thus the mark-up system may cause the franchisees to mistrust the franchisor. Since the franchise system is based largely on mutual trust between the two parties this is a disastrous situation which will rapidly lead to declining relations. The problem is further compounded if the franchisees fear that the franchisor can raise prices at will. For these reasons the services fee method is much more widely used than the mark-up system.

Fixed and minimum franchise fees

Fixed fees

This system of simply paying a fixed periodic fee is rarely used in practice. This is because the franchisee may struggle in the early days and the fixed fee may have been set at a level which he cannot afford to pay. On the other hand, the franchisor will not be able to participate in the increased business of his franchisees later on in the same way as he would have done if a fee based on turnover had applied.

Minimum fees

Occasionally a franchisor will wish to structure his ongoing fee system on a percentage management services fee basis but with a minimum fee payable. This may be justifiable provided the level of that minimum fee is relatively modest and represents, when grossed-up, the break-even performance of a typical franchisee in the network.

Charges for equipment purchased through the franchisor

Obviously the franchisee will need to purchase some equipment in order to operate his outlet. He may be able to buy such equipment from whatever supplier he wishes, or he may be contractually obliged to purchase from (or through) the franchisor. Franchisors often insist that they themselves arrange the supply of all necessary equipment in order to maintain uniform standards and/or so that they can add a mark-up to the price of the equipment and thereby increase their income. Some franchisors on the other hand resist the temptation to add a mark-up and instead decide to sell the equipment to the franchisees at cost on the basis that the increased goodwill that will result is worth more than any mark-up. However, the franchisor is usually in a position to be able to negotiate very good terms with suppliers and may therefore be able to earn a margin on the sale of equipment while still selling to franchisees at a lower price than they themselves could obtain independently. In the interest of goodwill it may be advisable for the franchisor to disclose to franchisees the margin that he is making on any such sales.

Some franchisors do not get directly involved in the sale of equipment but may 'introduce' franchisees to suppliers in return for a commission. Once again it is good practice that any such commission should be disclosed to the franchisee.

In other instances the whole franchise concept may be based on a specialized piece of equipment for which the franchisor holds the patent. In this case the franchisee will obviously be obliged to buy the equipment from the franchisor. The franchise may in fact have been specifically set up as a vehicle through which the franchisor can exploit his invention.

Leasing charges paid for premises/equipment

The franchisor may provide a leasing facility for franchisees so that they do not need to buy equipment or premises outright. This will significantly lower the amount of initial capital that the franchisee requires, and should therefore bring the franchise within the financial range of a greater number of potential franchisees, while at the same time providing the franchisor with additional income. Leasing will reduce the financial risk faced by franchisees since they will have to borrow less funds.

Alternatively, the franchisor might not actually provide the leasing facility himself but may introduce franchisees to a finance house in return for which he may receive a commission (which should be disclosed to the franchisee).

In many cases the owner of the premises used by the franchisee will insist that the franchisor leases the property, since the franchisee is seen as a greater risk. The franchisor will then sub-let the property to the franchisee.

Alternatively, the franchisor may actually own the property and will therefore earn rental income from the franchisee.

Contributions to an advertising fund

Franchise agreements usually require the franchisee to make some contribution to a central advertising and promotional fund. (The franchisor guarantees to spend all such funds on promotional activities.) Advertising funds are almost invariably raised by levying an additional charge on turnover, over and above the management services fees described above. In some cases a two-tier structure may operate whereby the franchisee pays into the central fund some small percentage of his turnover which the franchisor spends on national advertising, and in addition to this the franchisee must also undertake to spend a further amount on local advertising.

Alternatively, the franchisor may charge a percentage of the franchisee's gross income rather than turnover, or a fixed annual fee may be charged instead of a percentage.

6

Checklist

---

1. In addition to the usual expenses incurred when a business is established, stock, working capital, etc., franchisees will usually also have to pay to the franchisor:
   - an initial fee.
   - continuing fees in the form of either (a) a management services fee based on turnover, or (b) a mark-up on materials bought from the franchisor.
   - a contribution to a central advertising fund.
2. Franchisees may also have to pay the franchisor
   - for equipment bought from the franchisor.
   - leasing fees or rent on equipment and property belonging to the franchisor.
3. The justification for the taking of mark-ups and benefits in these areas by the franchisor has to be considered in the overall context of what the franchisee retains after all his fees and deductions and the franchisor's total income.

---

7 Raising the finance for a franchise

The clearing banks □ Franchise finance packages □ Bank facilities available to franchisees □ Non-scheme finance □ The Small Firms Loan Guarantee Scheme □ How to approach the banks – preparing a business plan □ Checklist

The clearing banks

Most of the major clearing banks have recognized the increasing importance of franchising in the 1980s and they now provide the bulk of external finance available to franchises.

In July 1981 National Westminster became the first bank to appoint a franchise manager within its Small Business Section, and since then it has loaned some £70 million to franchisees. Many of the banks have now introduced special franchise finance schemes which are primarily aimed at providing funding for potential franchisees.

All of the major banks have followed roughly the same approach of initially appointing a specialist franchise manager who provides advice and assistance to local branch managers. Thus when a potential franchisee approaches his local bank with a proposal to borrow funds in order to purchase a franchise, the local branch manager will consult the bank's franchise manager at head office. Since the franchise manager has considerable expertise in the franchising field he can quickly assess whether a specific proposition appears to be viable, and can provide the local branch manager with some basic information about the main features of the franchising system in general. The final decision to lend or not to lend money to any particular applicant is not taken by the franchise manager but by the local branch manager. This approach to the lending decision benefits from both the specialized expertise of the franchise manager and the branch manager's knowledge of specific local trading conditions and his assessment of the suitability of both the individual applicant and the proposed location for the franchise.

The banks are reassured by the knowledge that the franchisor will be as concerned as they themselves are that the franchisee succeeds – a failed franchise will be extremely detrimental to the franchisor's corporate image and the bank can therefore be confident that the franchisor will closely monitor his franchisees to try to ensure that their outlets are successful.

Franchise finance packages

All of the large banks are willing to arrange special franchise finance packages which are developed in co-operation with specific franchisors. These franchise packages are tailor-made to meet the requirements of potential franchisees who are intending to purchase an outlet from the franchisor concerned. The franchisor will automatically refer potential franchisees who are seeking financing to the bank with which the franchise package has been arranged.

Advantages of finance packages

Because the bank is familiar with the individual operations of these franchisors an application for a loan by one of their potential franchisees is usually dealt with more rapidly, and possibly on more favourable terms than a similar application for funds to buy an outlet from a franchisor who is unknown to the bank. From the franchisor's point of view being able to offer potential franchisees a special financing scheme is an extremely useful marketing aid:

- it assists the franchisees in securing the necessary financing with the minimum of fuss and formalities.
- it enables franchisees to obtain finance on terms which are normally reserved for the larger customer or concern.
- the franchisor knows that he has a ready source of finance for his franchisees provided they meet the outline parameters agreed between the franchisor and the bank.

Favourable terms for franchisees

The banks acknowledge that franchisees in a soundly constructed franchise are a lower credit risk than totally independent businessmen and are therefore prepared to lend on much more favourable terms to franchisees than they are to independents. Mr Tony Dutfield, Director of the BFA, claims that 12–14 per cent of franchisees fail within five years of starting compared to 90 per cent for independent small business start-ups.

The lower failure rate means that banks tend to

- lend franchisees more, and
- charge less interest
- sometimes accept less security for loans.

Most franchisees can borrow up to 70 per cent of their total start-up requirements, as opposed to approximately 50 per cent for an independent businessman. It would be undesirable to lend a greater proportion than this because the business may then be unable to generate sufficient cashflow to service the debt.

Franchisees are usually able to negotiate lower interest rates than those charged for independent start-ups. The average rate is usually 2.5 – 4 per cent above the bank's base lending rate. This is approximately 1 per cent below the rate charged on a normal small business start-up loan. Loans can be on either a fixed or a floating rate basis. Most of the franchise finance schemes permit a one- or two-year holiday on capital repayments on loans over £15 000. This can prove to be extremely useful to franchisees in the first few months when there tends to be a continuing net cash outflow.

Generally there will be a more flexible attitude on security requirements also to reflect the lower risk considered to be involved.

The period of the loan will be determined largely by the duration of the franchise agreement – e.g. if the agreement lasts for five years then ideally the bank would be looking for clearance within that term, although it is prepared to be flexible and will consider extending the term to seven, or even ten years provided the agreement is renewable without onerous conditions.

Bank control checks

The banks may require the franchisee to submit monthly management figures so that the actual performance that is achieved can be measured against the forecasted results for that month. Any variances between actual and planned performance can often be an invaluable early warning signal of impending problems. The banks may also require the franchisee to give his written authority allowing full information disclosure between the franchisor and the bank. Thus the bank can alert the franchisor if it feels that a franchisee is getting into difficulties. Naturally the franchisee may initially be less than enthusiastic about the idea of both the franchisor and the bank having full access to information relating to his financial position, but this system is intended to be beneficial to all three parties including the franchisee, since it should result in expedient identification and resolution of problems.

Bank facilities available to franchisees

Many banks insist on 'key-man' life insurance to protect their investment against the consequences of illness or death of the franchisee.

A franchisee can finance part of his operation through leasing and hire purchase. These services, which will usually be offered by the banks, are particularly useful if the franchisee is unable to purchase assets outright because he lacks sufficient capital and does not have adequate security to offer for a loan.

Non-scheme finance

Franchisees should not necessarily be put off if there is no specific franchise finance package in place. This may be for a number of reasons, including level of start-up costs, maturity of the franchise network, etc. The banks will maintain a comprehensive library of information on all known franchises in the UK and this information will be available to branch managers whenever they require it. However, in these instances the franchisee would normally approach the branch manager direct for assistance rather than through the franchisor and the bank's franchise department. Moreover, no specific guidelines will be laid down as to interest rates, start-up contribution, etc.

The Small Firms Loan Guarantee Scheme

Franchisees can benefit from the Small Firms Loan Guarantee Scheme (LGS) which was introduced by the Government in 1981. The objective of the scheme is to assist both existing businesses and viable but as yet untried new ventures which appear to have good potential but lack either adequate security or the sort of track record that is usually necessary in order to raise medium-term loans on normal commercial terms.

Terms of the LGS

Under the scheme the Government will provide lenders with a guarantee for 70 per cent of any approved loan. This guarantee facilitates borrowing for businesses which might otherwise be turned down because they are seen as being too much of a credit risk. In return for the guarantee the borrower pays a quarterly premium to the Government over and above the interest paid to the lender. This premium is currently 2.5 per cent per annum of the reducing amount guaranteed. Sole traders, partnerships, and limited companies are all eligible for the scheme. Whilst there is no formal upper limit on the size of company that can benefit from the scheme, large companies will not usually be considered. Most types of business are eligible (including retailing). Funds that are borrowed can be used to finance either fixed assets or working capital and the term of the loan must be between two and seven years.

Aim of the scheme

The whole purpose of the scheme is to encourage the setting-up and expansion of new businesses by providing a mechanism whereby firms are able to attract loans to which they would otherwise not have access because they are unable to offer adequate security. Provided that the lending bank is satisfied that the borrower's proposition is a viable one, but it is one that the bank could not agree to without the benefit of the Government guarantee, then an application can be made for help under the scheme. Because 70 per cent of the loan is guaranteed by the Government it clearly represents a fairly low credit risk to the lending banks, and they are therefore prepared to offer very favourable interest rates. For example, at the time of writing, National Westminster will offer loans that are guaranteed under the scheme at an interest rate of 1.75 per cent above base rate. In addition to the bank's interest charges there is the premium which must be paid to the Government. At 2.5 per cent on 70 per cent of the loan (i.e. the proportion which can be guaranteed) this works out at an additional premium of 1.75 per cent per annum on the total amount of the loan. Thus the total cost of the loan would be 3.5 per cent above base rate, which is an extremely favourable rate for a borrower with little security.

Franchises qualify for the Loan Guarantee Scheme. Many franchisees have taken advantage of it and have found it an invaluable help in raising the finance needed in order to open their units.

How to approach the banks – preparing a business plan

Whether or not there is a special financing package agreed with the banks the franchisee should prepare or have prepared for him a detailed Business Plan. Presenting a good case to the bank manager is the best possible step to obtaining the business finance required. Nothing impresses the banker more than a well thought out case with all the relevant facts properly marshalled and clearly presented. (*Starting Up* and *A Business Plan*, both published in this series, offer useful advice.) No two plans are identical – each one must be tailored to fit the specific characteristics of the proposed venture or franchise. However, there are certain pieces of information which will tend to appear in the majority of good franchise business plans and these can be summarized below:

- *Personal details of applicant/s*
  Address, marital status, dependants, education, work experience, respective salaries, etc.
  Financial information – bank and branch, with asset/liability synopsis (e.g. cash, value of home (less mortgage), savings, shares, other assets/liabilities).
- *Business background*
  Development and establishment of franchisor, together with market status, etc., details of product with unique features highlighted, number of employees in a typical outlet.
- *Start-up cost schedule*
  Breakdown of initial costs (e.g. initial franchise fee, equipment, shopfitting, legal fees) and working capital (overdraft) requirement.
- *Site details/evaluation*
  Brief synopsis of lease/freehold – address, lease term, rent review, premium, rates, area of shop.
  Local factors – prime/secondary site, competition within area, market potential (statistics), etc.
  Assessment of area as a whole and number of years business established in area (if appropriate).
- *Three-year cashflow forecast*
  Including loan repayment, interest, drawings, etc., together with explanatory notes re credit terms, leasing/HP details.
- *Projected three-year P & L accounts/balance sheet*
- *Audited accounts*
  Preferably for last three years at least (if appropriate) in cases of established/trading outlets.

Checklist

- Finance for franchisees can be raised from the clearing banks through either (1) special finance packages, or
    (2) on a non-scheme basis.
- Finance is available on overdraft, fixed rate loan, variable rate loan or through the Government's Small Firms Loan Guarantee Scheme.
- The lending proposition should be presented in the form of a comprehensive Business Plan.

7

8 The British Franchise Association and other sources of advice

The British Franchise Association □ Membership of the BFA □ The BFA Code of Ethics □ The BFA as a source of information □ Other sources of advice – BFA affiliate members □ Franchise brokers □ Professional financial and legal advice □ Government sources of information and advice

The British Franchise Association

The British Franchise Association is an organization of franchisors which came into existence in December 1977. It was set up by the following eight well-established companies who were actively franchising in the UK at that time:

Prontaprint Ltd.
Dyno-Rod Ltd.
Wimpy International Ltd.
Kentucky Fried Chicken (GB) Ltd.
Budget Rent a Car (UK) Ltd.
Service Master Ltd.
Ziebart Mobile Transport Services Ltd.
Holiday Inns (UK) Ltd.

The BFA was originally set up in order to serve two main purposes:

(a) To act as a trade association to represent and promote the interests of the franchising industry.
(b) To try to disassociate reputable franchisors from pyramid selling operations which had proliferated in the late 1960s and early 1970s.

One of the main objectives of the BFA is to establish 'a clear definition of the ethical franchising standards to assist members of the public, press, potential investors and Government bodies in differentiating between sound business opportunities and any suspect investment offers.' In short, the BFA aims to act as a representative body for the franchising industry as a whole by providing information and education on the subject (through press releases, conferences and seminars), and to serve as the collective voice of the industry in liaison with Government departments and foreign franchise organizations.

Membership of the BFA

The Association operates a dual membership system, consisting of both 'full members' and 'qualified non-members'. In order to qualify as a full member a franchisor must have successfully operated a pilot scheme for at least one year and must have a minimum of four franchisees, at least two of which must have been in operation for not less than two years. A franchisor who is unable to meet these criteria may instead apply to become a qualified non-member, provided that he has operated a pilot scheme for one year and has at least one franchisee who has been in operation for not less than one year. In December 1988 the BFA had 90 full members and 29 qualified non-members. The qualified non-members are not considered to have fully proved themselves in the marketplace yet, and are therefore 'on probation'. Franchisors who are classified as qualified non-members will receive the benefit of BFA advice, and will be invited to attend seminars, conferences etc., thereby benefiting from contact with more experienced full members. Non-qualified members will be admitted to full membership once they meet the criteria listed above.

8

The BFA Code of Ethics

All members, whether 'full' or 'non-qualified', must abide by the Code of Ethics which was introduced by the BFA in 1978, and which has remained unchanged ever since. This is a ten point code 'for the proper business conduct of franchisors' and is intended to protect franchisees (both existing and potential) from unscrupulous practices by franchisors. The important requirements of the code include that:

- no member shall mislead or deceive franchisees
- all material information shall be disclosed before a contract is signed
- the form and content of any franchise agreement be in compliance with approved practice
- franchisors select franchisees carefully
- franchisors supervise their franchisees' activities

- the franchisor will act fairly and in good faith when dealing with franchisees.

Franchisors who are found guilty of breaches of the code are liable to be expelled from the BFA. The full Code of Ethics is given below:

BFA Code of Ethics*

1 The BFA's Code of Advertising Practice shall be based on that established by the Advertising Standards Association and shall be modified from time to time in accordance with alterations notified by the ASA.

The BFA will subscribe fully to the ASA Code unless, on some specific issue, it is resolved by a full meeting of the Council of the BFA that the ASA is acting against the best interests of the public and of franchising business in general on that specific issue. In this case the BFA will be required to formally notify the ASA, setting out the grounds for disagreement.

2 No member shall sell, offer for sale, or distribute any product or render any service, or promote the sale or distribution thereof, under any representation or condition (including the use of the name of a 'celebrity') which has the tendency, capacity, or effect of misleading or deceiving purchasers or prospective purchasers.

3 No member shall imitate the trademark, trade name, corporate identity, slogan, or other mark of identification of another franchisor in any manner or form that would have the tendency or capacity to mislead or deceive.

4 Full and accurate written disclosure of all information material to the franchise relationship shall be given to prospective franchisees within a reasonable time prior to the execution of any binding document.

5 The franchise agreement shall set forth clearly the respective obligations and responsibilities of the parties and all other terms of the relationship, and be free from ambiguity.

6 The franchise agreement and all matters basic and material to the arrangement and relationship thereby created, shall be in writing and executed copies thereof given to the franchisee.

7 A franchisor shall select and accept only those franchisees who, upon reasonable investigation, possess the basic skills, education, personal qualities, and adequate capital to succeed. There shall be no discrimination based on race, colour, religion, national origin or sex.

* Reproduced by permission of the British Franchise Association

8 A franchisor shall exercise reasonable surveillance over the activities of his franchisees to the end that the contractual obligations of both parties are observed and the public interest safeguarded.

9 Fairness shall characterize all dealings between a franchisor and its franchisees. A franchisor shall give notice to its franchisee of any contractual breach and grant reasonable time to remedy default.

10 A franchisor shall make every effort to resolve complaints, grievances and disputes with its franchisees with good faith and good will through fair and reasonable direct communication and negotiation.

The BFA as a source of information

One of the major functions of the BFA is in dealing with the many thousands of enquiries that it receives every year from potential franchisees, the general public, the press, academics, etc. requesting advice or information. (NB the BFA makes information available not only about its members but also about other franchisors who are not connected with the Association, where appropriate.) Arguably this is one of the most important aspects of the BFA's work. The Association is an excellent source of information for anyone interested in franchising and has been a major force in increasing public awareness and understanding of the franchise system. The BFA has sponsored many promotional and investigative activities, including the National Franchise Exhibition which is held annually in London.

In March 1986 the BFA launched its 'Early Development Service'. A fee of £550 + VAT provides access to a variety of services (both legal and financial), plus a half-day counselling session with the Chairman of the Association. A two-day seminar on all aspects of the industry and four 'theme' lunches on several topics are also provided, and twice a year a BFA lawyer and treasurer hold surgeries for individual counselling sessions.

The BFA will continue to play an invaluable role in the franchising industry so long as it continues to ensure that franchisors are only admitted to membership once they have proved themselves to be responsible operators. The Association must also be seen to be strictly enforcing compliance by its members with the Code of Ethics (both in principle and in spirit) and it should continue to attempt to anticipate the development of any undesirable practices and take whatever preventative action is needed in order to discourage any such developments. If these goals are upheld then the BFA will maintain its good reputation, and will continue to be heard as 'the voice of responsible franchising'.

At present the BFA is highly respected as the unified body of UK franchising. Membership of the BFA is seen as a positive indication of a franchisor's reputation and is therefore a powerful marketing aid when selling a franchise. Hence the Association provides a strong incentive for franchisors to act responsibly so that they will be accepted as members.

Other sources of advice – BFA affiliate members

In addition to its franchisor members the BFA also grants 'affiliate membership' to non-franchise organizations who play an active role in the industry, including lawyers, accountants, banks etc. The BFA's affiliate membership listing as at December 1988 was as follows:

Area of business	Number
Solicitors	13
Chartered accountants	9
Franchise consultants	6
Bankers	9
Insurance brokers	1
Exhibition organizers	1
Chartered surveyors	3
Patent and trade mark agents	1

In order to be admitted to the BFA affiliate listing an applicant must demonstrate an understanding of the franchising system, provide references from two full members describing successfully concluded contracts or arrangements, be approved by the BFA's Council and must undertake to abide by the Association's Code of Ethics.

Franchise brokers

Recent additions to the range of advisory services which are available within the franchise industry include a number of franchisee recruitment services and notably the first official franchise brokerage in the UK. A franchise broker usually operates by circulating to prospective franchisees a list of franchises that are currently available. The broker earns his fee in the form of a commission for bringing the two parties together. Franchise brokers are generally frowned upon in the UK, which helps to explain why there are so few of them. It is argued that brokers who are paid on a commission basis may be too keen to sell a franchise to the first potential franchisee who comes along, with possibly disastrous consequences for both the franchisee and the franchisor later on.

Professional financial and legal advice

It should go without saying that nobody should enter into an agreement to buy, or sell, a franchise without first taking professional financial and legal advice.

A good accountant should be able to advise a prospective franchisee whether the franchisor's projections of turnover, profit etc. for the proposed outlet appear to be feasible, how much the franchisee should be prepared to pay for the outlet, how best to raise the necessary finance, how to minimize his tax bill, etc. Several of the accountancy firms have developed an interest in franchising, and are affiliated with the BFA. Their interest lies primarily in providing financial advice for franchisors in areas such as preparation of business plans for franchisors, cash flow/ profitability forecasts, and taxation work. However, they should be just as willing to assist franchisees.

There are also several firms of solicitors who offer specialist advice on franchising. An investment in the advice of such specialists will be well worth while since a mistake or misunderstanding which is not clarified before the franchise contract is signed may prove to be extremely expensive, if not impossible, to rectify at a later date.

The BFA are always willing to provide a list of addresses of specialists in both the financial and legal aspects of franchising.

Government sources of information and advice

8

There are a wide range of free Government information sources available to anyone considering entering the franchise industry. These include the Department of Employment's Small Firms Service which is a free information and business counselling service. Unfortunately, most of the information that is widely available tends to be aimed at small business in general and there is not a great deal of published information specifically about franchising. This lack of specific information further increases the importance of the BFA as an advisory body.

For further information contact: British Franchise Association, Franchise Chambers, Thames View, Newtown Road, Henley-on-Thames, Oxon, RG9 1HG. Tel: (0491) 578049.

9   Problems in the franchise relationship

Motivation and satisfaction at work □ Franchisee dissatisfaction and the franchise relationship 'life cycle' □ Strategies for avoiding dissatisfaction – franchisee selection □ Joint consultative committees □ Franchisee associations □ Successful problem management □ Checklist

Many of the problems which develop in the relationship between the franchisee and the franchisor are related to the level of psychological satisfaction that is experienced by the franchisee. It is therefore useful to gain an insight into what factors are likely to motivate somebody to become a franchisee, and the possible changes in motivation and satisfaction which may occur over time.

Motivation and satisfaction at work

Security

It would seem reasonable to suggest that in most cases employee status will offer greater job security than self-employment. Consequently an individual who has a high psychological need for security and stability is most likely to feel happy and satisfied in a secure job working for somebody else. Such a person is unlikely to be motivated to take the risks associated with starting a business of his own.

Having said that, many of the risks related to starting a business can be avoided by buying a franchise. Therefore an individual who is prepared to take some limited degree of risk may well find that he would enjoy the satisfaction of running a business of his own in the form of a franchised outlet and thereby avoiding the inherent insecurity associated with 'going-it-alone'.

Team spirit

A second factor which influences the degree of satisfaction experienced at work is the extent to which a person is afforded the opportunity to feel as though he is part of a team. Some people derive great satisfaction from a work environment where there is a strong team spirit. This sort of person is most likely to be happy working in a large organization rather than starting his own one-man operation where he may have limited close contact with others. At the other extreme there are the 'loners' who much prefer to keep themselves to themselves and derive little satisfaction from working in a large team.

In between these two extremes lies the person who would derive most satisfaction from working on his own, or with only a small team, so long as he could experience a sense of belonging to some sort of larger team. A franchise may well be the ideal solution for such a person since the team spirit is (or at least should be) provided by the feeling of being an integral part of the franchise network, and the sense of identity with other franchisees.

Self-esteem

A third factor which contributes towards job satisfaction is the feeling of self-esteem and achievement provided by the work situation. Many people who have a high need for self-esteem and achievement find that they are unable to satisfy this need so long as they are an employee. They experience the feeling of being merely a small cog in a large machine and that their actions and efforts are not necessarily given the recognition which they feel they deserve. Self-employment on the other hand is usually associated with a feeling of greater self-esteem, autonomy, and recognition. Society currently places great value on entrepreneurialism and this is probably one of the major reasons why some people opt out of employee status in order to set up a business of their own. Therefore someone who is initially an employee may find that he is attracted by the idea of buying a franchise as this would increase his autonomy, power, etc. Thus the move from employee status into self-employment, whether totally independent or as a franchisee, will often prove to be an extremely satisfying experience.

The 'ideal' franchisee

Having considered the implications of the various levels of psychological need we might now describe the 'ideal' franchisee, from a psychological theory viewpoint, as an individual who has moderate needs for security, affiliation, esteem and autonomy. Somebody with very high needs for security and affiliation might be happier as an employee, while someone with a particularly strong need for autonomy might be better suited to independent self-employment, free from any controls such as those imposed by a franchisor.

There must be many people who are presently employees who feel a sense of frustration and a lack of fulfilment in their job, but who do not possess the psychological characteristics which are needed in order to 'make the break' and set up their own independent business. In other words many people have a psychological make-up which lies in the middle ground between the risk-taking entrepreneur and the security-seeking employee. Many franchisors recognize this fact, as can be seen in the approach that they adopt in their advertisements – they do not necessarily try to sell their particular franchise operation on the basis of its relative merits, but instead emphasize the psychological benefit of 'being your own boss' and they stress the advantages of franchising in general as a route into self-employment.

Franchisee dissatisfaction and the franchise relationship 'life cycle'

Most people who become franchisees will initially be extremely content with their new venture and will derive much greater satisfaction through operating their new outlet than they could possibly have hoped to experience as an employee. However, the degree of satisfaction experienced by the franchisee will not necessarily constantly remain at such a high level over a prolonged period of time and in fact may often decrease within a relatively short time-span. Therefore there may be some sort of 'life cycle' in the relationship between the franchisee and the franchisor. This can lead to serious problems for both parties. The solutions to many of these problems lie mainly with the franchisor who should be aware from the outset of the causes of franchisee discontent so that he can take whatever steps are necessary either to prevent this situation arising in the first place, or to implement a system capable of dealing with the problem if and when it occurs.

Control

The main cause of franchisee dissatisfaction stems from the fact that many franchisees, once they have successfully operated their outlet for a while, begin to resent both the continuing control exerted over them by the franchisor and the fact that they have to pay continuing services fees. They feel that their success is due entirely to their own efforts and they soon forget about the vital help which the franchisor provided when they first started. Thus while the franchise may temporarily satisfy their need for self-esteem and autonomy, the continuing control which is exerted by the franchisor may rapidly reduce the franchisee's feeling of autonomy. The franchisee may eventually feel no better off in this respect than he did as an employee. For most franchisees an increasing need for autonomy will develop as they gain confidence and experience. Consequently the gap between the level of autonomy that they desire and the degree of freedom and control that they are actually afforded may continue to widen. In this

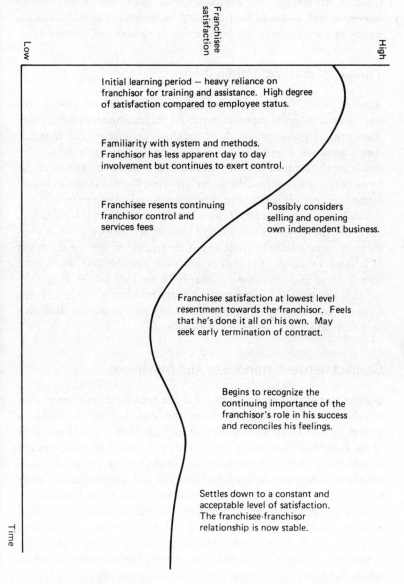

Fig. 9.1 Franchisee satisfaction and the 'life cycle' of the franchisee relationship

case the feeling of dissatisfaction may become so strong that the franchisee feels stifled by the control that is exerted over him by the franchisor and he may therefore seek to terminate the franchise relationship in order to 'go it alone'. In other cases the franchisee may go through a phase where he experiences dissatisfaction for a short while but he then manages to reconcile his feelings and appreciates that this control is in his own interest as well as that of the franchisor (as shown in Fig. 9.1). Thus the feeling of dissatisfaction may be either permanent or only temporary.

Threats of contract termination

Another major source of franchisee dissatisfaction can arise if the franchisor attempts to suppress or control the franchisees by threatening them with termination of their franchise agreement. All franchise contracts include a termination clause giving the franchisor the right to terminate the contract if the franchisee fails to adhere strictly to all the terms of the agreement, on the grounds that any deviation from stipulated terms may result in a lack of standardization and consequently a loss of goodwill. In practice the franchisor will usually find that it is fairly easy to prove that the franchisee has diverged from the terms of the contract, even if only in some relatively trivial way. If the franchisor does use the threat of termination against franchisees then their psychological need for the feeling of security may not necessarily be satisfied in the long term through the franchise relationship. Clearly franchisors can reduce this source of discontent by refraining from using the termination clause as a stick with which to threaten the franchisee.

Conflict between franchisor and franchisee

Because of the continuing control that the franchisor must exert over franchisees in order to ensure uniform standards, there will inevitably be certain areas in which the objectives of the franchisee diverge from those of the franchisor and consequently there are bound to be some areas of conflict between the two parties. It is unrealistic to expect to be able to achieve total harmony between the franchisor and the franchisees – some conflict is unavoidable, and could even be argued to be beneficial in moderation as it may help to ensure that the franchise relationship remains dynamic and might prevent it from becoming staid and uninteresting. However, the degree of any such conflict should be closely monitored. Unmanaged conflict can rapidly develop into a severe problem. The franchisor must therefore develop a system that will keep the level of conflict, and consequently any franchisee dissatisfaction, under control and he should try to ensure that the objectives and aspirations of both parties coincide with one another.

Strategies for avoiding dissatisfaction – franchisee selection

The first and most obvious way of avoiding the build-up of excessive franchisee dissatisfaction lies in careful initial selection of franchisees. The franchisor should develop some sort of 'ideal franchisee profile' against which prospective franchisees should be compared in order to determine whether they appear to be suitable candidates, although it is important to realize that such a profile can be used only as a rough guide as to the sort of qualities and characteristics that the franchisor should look for. He cannot expect individual franchisees to precisely match his 'ideal' profile. For example, the franchisor should not sell franchises to individuals who are strongly independent since they would soon begin to resent the control which the franchisor would exert over them and consequently dissatisfaction would rapidly develop. Furthermore, if these franchisees turned out to be opinion leaders amongst their contemporaries they might also breed discontent amongst their peers. This may seem an obvious point, but many franchisors have made the mistake of selling franchises to such people – the temptation to do so may be particularly great when the franchise system is first set up since the franchisor will understandably be very keen to make his first sale, and he might not be as selective in his choice of franchisee as he really ought to be. This situation can be disastrous if the franchisee begins to 'rebel' before the franchisor has been able to debug the system as a whole and may lead to the collapse of the entire franchise operation.

The franchisor can attempt to prevent the development of dissatisfaction by constantly reminding the franchisee of the importance of the continuing role which he plays in the franchisee's success, although he should try to be subtle in the way he sets about this task! This will often 'bring around' a dissatisfied franchisee who will then settle down to running his business.

The franchisor may also attempt to anticipate and avoid the problem of dissatisfaction by offering a franchisee the opportunity of opening a second franchise once he has fully mastered the operation of his first outlet. Hopefully this will maintain the franchisee's interest and at the same time remind him that the franchisor does indeed play a significant role in his continuing operation. This sort of strategy would be based upon the premise that as a result of being the owner of more than one outlet the franchisee will experience an increased feeling of satisfaction and independence along with reduced frustration at the level of control that is exercised by the franchisor.

Joint consultative committees

Many franchisors have acknowledged that there may be an imbalance in the relative power of the two parties to the franchise agreement and have anticipated the dissatisfaction that this may cause amongst franchisees. One way of trying to limit or avoid this dissatisfaction is by means of a 'joint consultative committee'.

A joint consultative committee consists of representatives of both the franchisor and the franchisees. Ideally the franchisees' representative should be elected by the franchisees themselves rather than being selected by the franchisor. The explicit objectives of these committees are usually to:

- promote two-way communications
- involve franchisees in decision making
- encourage feedback, not only of complaints but also of opinions and suggestions concerning new and existing products or operating methods.

In other words they are promoted as being a way of giving franchisees greater collective bargaining power with the franchisor and the chance to have a say in the operation of the franchise organization.

Problems with joint consultative committees

Representation

Whilst in theory joint consultative committees are undoubtedly commendable, in practice they do not always work quite as well as they should. Part of the problem stems from the fact that in electing a representative, franchisees tend to choose their more successful and well-established counterparts because they feel that these individuals will have greater influence with the franchisor than some of the smaller franchisees. Whilst it is true that these franchisees do indeed have more influence, this very fact means that they are often in a strong enough position to look after their own interests on a one-to-one basis with the franchisor. Consequently they may have only limited personal interest in the success of a joint consultative committee. Furthermore, their problems and interests may be quite different from those of their smaller and less well-established counterparts. Indeed their interests may lie closer to those of the franchisor than to the other franchisees. It is therefore essential that the interests of all franchisees are represented on the joint consultative committee if it is to serve any useful purpose as a 'collective bargaining' tool.

Little real influence

A further problem with joint consultative committees is that they may be used by the franchisor as little more than a tension management device. In other words his real objective is to prevent a build-up of franchisee dissatisfaction by setting up a committee in order to give the franchisees the impression that they have some real involvement in decision making, whereas in reality little attention may be paid to the comments raised by the committee. Therefore in some, but by no means all, cases joint consultative committees serve a primarily cosmetic function, and are viewed by the franchisor as a means of allowing the franchisees to 'let off steam'. They may serve a useful purpose from the franchisor's point of view in that they divert complaints away from the franchisor himself towards the franchisees' representative. It is certainly true that unless they are carefully organized joint consultative committees may be of little real benefit to the franchisees, and consequently may themselves be a further source of franchisee dissatisfaction!

Franchisee associations

Franchisee associations are organizations which are either established by the franchisor or occasionally by the franchisees themselves in order to provide a mechanism through which they can exert pressure on the franchisor via a unified body. They may also help to increase the feeling of affiliation amongst franchisees and at the same time provide a forum through which franchisees can discuss their mutual problems and benefit from each other's experiences. Franchisee associations are distinct from joint consultative committees in that they are usually totally independent of the franchisor who has little or no direct involvement in the association.

A franchisee association will often provide the best method of settling inter-franchisee disputes. For example, one franchisee may be 'raiding' employees from another franchisee. The affected parties may prefer to solve the problem through an association which is independent of the franchisor, who may have his 'pet' franchisees. This is a situation which the franchisor may also find desirable since it means that he can avoid getting involved in some of the more trivial disputes and he therefore does not have to make judgements which may result in accusations of favouritism.

Successful problem management

The franchisors who have been most successful in holding down the level of franchisee related problems have tended to be those who have recognized and anticipated the problems of franchisee dissatisfaction. They have therefore implemented an effective system of ensuring that franchisor-franchisee relations are maintained. This involves not only co-operating with franchisees through a joint consultative committee or franchisee association, but also maintaining personal contact with individual franchisees through an open-door policy and, most importantly, anticipation of potential sources of conflict and dissatisfaction.

The franchise relationship is a two-sided affair and each party must be prepared to take account of the changing needs and demands of the other. Problems should be anticipated and avoided wherever possible, and those which do arise should be dealt with on an amicable basis. It is vital that the relationship does not deteriorate into an 'us and them' situation.

Checklist

1. The 'ideal' franchisee can be seen as someone with moderate needs for:
   * security
   * affiliation
   * self-esteem
   * autonomy.
2. Franchisee dissatisfaction can arise because of:
   * resentment of the continuing control of the franchisor
   * threatened termination of the franchise contract by the franchisor.
3. Dissatisfaction can be moderated by:
   * careful franchisee selection
   * allowing established franchisees to open other outlets
   * the use of joint consultative committees, provided that they (a) represent all franchisees, (b) do have real influence
   * the use of franchisee associations.

10 The franchise contract

Description of the franchise □ Duration of the franchise contract □ Leases □ Territorial rights □ Initial and continuing fees payable by the franchisee □ Contractual obligations of the franchisor □ Contractual obligations of the franchisee □ Termination of the contract by either party □ The franchisee's right to assign the business □ The purchase agreement and the franchise agreement □ Checklist

The franchise contract is clearly an extremely important document from both parties' point of view. It should include all the terms of the agreement and the obligations of each party, which together define the relationship between the franchisee and the franchisor. The franchisee should not enter into any formal agreement without first consulting a solicitor, preferably one who is a specialist in the field of franchising, to ensure that he fully understands the implications of all the terms which are included in the agreement. The cost involved in seeking specialist advice may well prove to be one of the best investments that the franchisee ever makes.

The franchisor will usually have a standard contract which he will offer every franchisee. The specific terms which are included in a franchise contract will of course vary from one franchise operation to the next, but there are certain terms which will be common to the vast majority of agreements. Some of the more important considerations are outlined in this chapter.

One of the most important points to bear in mind when evaluating a franchise contract is that all terms, obligations, etc. should be put down in writing in order to avoid any argument at a later date. If the franchisor has fully thought out his operation, then all terms should have already been incorporated into the standard contract. Consequently most franchisors will not be prepared to negotiate special terms with individual franchisees. The contract should leave no ambiguities which might later lead to disputes between the two parties.

Description of the franchise

Most contracts will start with a brief description of the franchise that is being sold. Details will be given outlining the operation, the trade marks, trade names, know-how, copyright and systems that are involved and who owns the rights to them. These are known as intellectual property rights.

Duration of the franchise contract

The duration of the initial franchise agreement must be long enough to allow the franchisee to recoup his initial investment in the operation, i.e. the front-end fee and his investment in equipment, shop-fitting and so on. Consequently the initial term should normally be no less than five years for a business format franchise. The franchisee should also be granted an option to renew the agreement on expiry of this initial term, provided of course that he has fulfilled his contractual obligations during the initial period. The conditions relating to renewal of the agreement should be clearly specified in the contract. It would be unusual for the franchisee to be required to pay a second 'front-end' fee on renewal. If the franchisee exercises his option to renew the agreement, this will often be on the understanding that the contract that will govern the second period will be that which is offered to new franchisees at the date of renewal. Thus the franchisee may find that the obligations of both parties after renewal would be slightly different from those which prevailed during the initial period.

One other consideration relating to the term of the agreement is that the franchisee will usually be obliged to carry out periodic redecoration, renovation, etc. in order to maintain the appearance and image of his outlet. He may also be obliged from time to time to invest in new equipment. The franchisee should assure himself that any such periodic obligations are neither unreasonable nor excessive.

Leases

If the franchisor either owns the premises from which the franchisee will operate, or is sub-letting them to the franchisee, then the duration of the lease should be the same as that of the franchise agreement. Furthermore, termination of the franchise agreement (by either party) should also automatically terminate the lease agreement.

Territorial rights

Many franchise agreements include an undertaking by the franchisor that he will not subsequently sell additional franchises within the defined territory in which the franchisee will operate. Such undertakings must be worded carefully so that they do not breach restrictive trade practices legislation. Whether or not such exclusive territorial rights are granted to the franchisee, it is not in the franchisor's long-term interest to over-saturate an area with more outlets than it can realistically support. Such action will inevitably lead to the failure of some, if not all of the outlets within that territory, and consequently the franchisor's image and goodwill will be diminished. If some sort of territorial rights are granted, then the franchisee should determine whether they are fixed for the duration of the agreement, or whether the franchisor can reduce or change the territory and, if so, under what conditions.

The franchisee will also often be required to restrict his operations to the designated territory in order to prevent him from 'poaching' business from other franchisees.

Initial and continuing fees payable by the franchisee

Naturally the contract will specify the payments that the franchisee is required to make to the franchisor in consideration for the granting of the right to operate a franchise. The level of the initial fee should be stated, along with a description of exactly what the franchisee will receive in return for this fee. The initial fee is usually payable in instalments, e.g. a deposit on signing the agreement, and subsequent payments as equipment is delivered, training is received, etc. The franchisor will normally require that the entire amount of the initial fee is paid before the franchisee commences trading. The timing of all payments should be specified, and it should be quite clear whether the cost of delivery and installation of equipment is included, and whether the quoted fee is inclusive or exclusive of VAT. The contract should also specify whether any part of the initial fee is refundable and, if so, under what conditions. For example, if during the pre-opening training it becomes apparent that the franchisee is unlikely to be able to operate his outlet effectively, then the franchisor may reserve the right at that stage to terminate the agreement. In this situation it would seem fair that the franchisee should be entitled to a full refund of any deposit that he has paid. However, if it is the franchisee who decides that he does not wish to proceed any further with the agreement, then the franchisor should be entitled to recover any reasonable expenses that he has so far incurred before refunding the balance of any deposit collected from the franchisee.

10

Continuing fee

Where applicable, the level of the continuing services fee to be paid by the franchisee should always be stated, along with the method by which this continuing fee will be calculated. The contract will usually specify that the franchisor reserves certain rights so that he can check that the franchisee is not deliberately under-declaring his turnover in order to evade full payment of services fees. Therefore the franchisor will probably reserve the right to make spot checks on the franchisee without prior warning, in order to check his stock levels, financial records, invoices from suppliers etc. The franchisee will also usually be required to use a standardized accounting system which will assist the franchisor in identifying franchisees who are under-performing, and those that he suspects might be under-declaring sales.

Mark-up

Instead of charging a continuing management services fee some franchisors add a mark-up to the price of goods sold to franchisees. In the interests of mutual trust it is advisable for the franchisor to disclose the level of any such mark-up to the franchisee, and the contract should somehow assure the franchisee that the franchisor is not able to increase the level of this mark-up indiscriminately. The franchisee should be wary of any clause which requires him to maintain at least some minimum purchase level, unless that minimum level is reasonable.

Advertising fund

The franchisee will inevitably be required to make some contribution to an advertising fund. Sometimes this is included in the continuing services fee based on turnover, and in other cases an additional charge is levied over and above this fee. Whichever method is used, the contract should state clearly not only what the franchisee's financial obligations are, but also the manner in which the franchisor undertakes to spend this fund, for example, what proportion will be spent on national advertising of the overall chain, and what proportion will be spent on regional advertising in order to promote the franchisee's individual outlet.

Contractual obligations of the franchisor

The franchisor's obligations should be described comprehensively in the contract. Examples of details which should be included are:

- the initial training which the franchisor undertakes to provide, such as
  - (a) what the training consists of
  - (b) how long it will last
  - (c) whether or not the franchisee has to make an additional payment for it
- whether the franchisor is obliged to provide assistance in locating a suitable site for the franchisee or not
- the franchisor's obligation to provide a comprehensive and understandable operating manual
- the continuing assistance which should be available to the franchisee, such as
  - (a) help in day-to-day managerial problems
  - (b) assistance in staff training
  - (c) provision of an accounting system
- the franchisor's obligation to grant the franchisee the right to use all of his trade marks, know-how, secret methods, etc.
- the franchisor's obligation to continue to supply the franchisee with the goods and services required in the operation of the outlet. If the supply cannot be maintained, the franchisee should be free to purchase similar quality substitutes independently.

Contractual obligations of the franchisee

The majority of the obligations which are imposed upon the franchisee are intended to ensure that the image and goodwill associated with the franchisor's trade marks and the overall franchise chain are maintained to a high standard. Therefore the franchisee will be subject to obligations which should ensure standardization in all franchised outlets. Consequently the franchise contract will stipulate that the franchisee will be obliged to:

10

- adhere to all the operating methods that have been demonstrated during the training period, along with those described in the operating manual
- maintain his outlet in a clean and sanitary state
- ensure that his staff are fully trained in the prescribed operating methods
- use the promotional material supfiled by the franchisor, along with any packaging, etc., used in the business
- maintain minimum opening hours.

The franchisee will also be prevented from undertaking his own promotional campaigns without first receiving the franchisor's approval.

Since the franchise contract is drawn up by the franchisor it will usually go to some length in specifying all the obligations that are imposed upon the franchisee. The franchisee must assure himself that these requirements are neither unreasonable nor excessively restrictive. For example, the franchisee must ascertain whether he is obliged to sell only those goods that he purchases from the franchisor. If this is the case, what assurance does he have that the franchisor will not charge an unrealistically high price for those goods, and what controls are there to prevent him from imposing persistent price increases? Similarly the franchisee must be sure that should he eventually wish to sell the business the franchisor cannot impose any unreasonable restrictions on the sale that would prevent him from securing a fair market price for his outlet.

Termination of the contract by either party

The contract should clearly state the conditions under which each party can terminate the contract prematurely. One of the franchisor's primary concerns is to maintain the value of his trade marks and the goodwill that he has established by ensuring that the franchisee adheres to stipulated operating methods. If the franchisee seriously deviates from standard procedure then he should initially be given a written warning from the franchisor. If, however, the franchisee persists in his failure to comply with required procedure then the franchisor may seek termination of the agreement. It is quite correct that the franchisor should retain this right, but the franchisee must be sure that the franchisor cannot terminate the relationship merely for a trivial breach of contract. If, however, the franchisee is guilty of some 'material' (i.e. very serious) breach, then it is not unreasonable of the franchisor to expect to be allowed to terminate the contract immediately. Examples of what might be considered to be a material breach of contract include:

- under-declaration of sales (to avoid services fee payments)
- purchasing goods from sources other than the franchisor himself (or his nominated suppliers)
- any act which would be likely to harm substantially the franchisor's goodwill.

The franchisee should also have the right to terminate the contract under certain specified conditions. For example, if the franchisor's forecasts relating to turnover, profit, etc. prove to have been substantially over-optimistic and therefore misleading, or if the franchisor consistently fails to provide the continuing services stipulated in the contract, then the franchisee may seek to terminate the agreement.

The rights of each party subsequent to premature termination should also be defined in the contract. Any financial penalties that either party may suffer should be specified.

The franchisee's right to assign the business

The franchisee should have the right to assign his business to a third party, subject to certain controls imposed by the franchisor. The contract will usually specify that the franchisor can veto the sale of the franchise to any individual who is unsuitable as a franchisee. The franchisee should not normally be allowed to sell his business to anyone unless they are prepared to undergo the franchisor's training programme and the purchaser will usually be obliged to pay the franchisor for providing any such training. Many agreements grant to the franchisor the right of first refusal should the franchisee wish to dispose of the business. However, the franchisee should be entitled to sell his business at its market value, and therefore if the franchisor does retain the right of first refusal the basis of valuation should also be stipulated. In many cases the franchisor will have a waiting list of franchisees who would be prepared to buy the outlet, in which case the franchisor may charge the franchisee some percentage of the selling price in consideration for arranging the sale.

After the franchisee has disposed of his business he will usually be prevented, by means of a restrictive covenant, from operating a similar business in competition with the franchisor or any of his franchisees for a specified period of time. Any such clause must not be unreasonably restrictive from the franchisee's point of view. He will of course be prevented from using any of the franchisor's trade marks, know-how, trade secrets, etc. after the relationship has been terminated.

10

In the unfortunate event of the franchisee's death the contract should make provision for his family to be able either to take over the business (after receiving adequate training from the franchisor) or to dispose of it at its market value. It is not uncommon for the franchisor to agree to manage the business (for a fee) until a suitable purchaser can be found.

The purchase agreement and the franchise agreement

The franchise contract will often be divided into two separate agreements. The first is described as a 'Purchase Agreement', and the second as the 'Franchise Agreement'. The purchase agreement is concerned with the relationship between the two parties prior to the commencement of trading by the prospective franchisee, whereas the franchise agreement relates to their respective obligations once the franchisee's outlet is actually in operation. The purchase agreement basically states that the franchisee intends to purchase a franchise and enter into a franchise agreement subject to the franchisor finding a suitable site and the franchisee being able to raise the necessary finance. A deposit will normally be payable by the franchisee on signing the purchase agreement. The franchisor will then begin searching for a suitable location, and the franchisee will approach the banks in order to secure sufficient funding. At this stage, before the franchise agreement has been signed, either party might, under certain specified circumstances, be able to back out of the agreement. For example, if the franchisor were unable to find a mutually acceptable site within a reasonable time period then the franchisee might be able to opt out of the arrangement and reclaim his deposit in full. If on the other hand the franchisee refused to accept what was effectively a suitable site then the relationship might end there, although the franchisee would probably be unable to reclaim his full deposit – the franchisor should be entitled to retain an amount sufficient to cover any reasonable expenses which he has incurred in connection with the purchase agreement. If, however, all goes well then the franchise agreement will be signed. This embodies all the obligations of each party concerning the operation of the outlet, its eventual disposal etc. Consequently the franchise agreement will be a much more substantial document than the purchase agreement.

Non-negotiability of the contract

The franchisor should resist the temptation to offer any special deals in order to secure the sale of a franchise as this is likely to lead to discontent among other franchisees at a later stage when they find out that somebody else has been given a better deal than them. Consequently, a franchisor who has thoroughly prepared his operation before offering it as a franchise should have drawn up a comprehensive contract, and should be unwilling to make any major modifications to it in response to demands from individual franchisees. The prospective franchisee should bear this in mind when negotiating with the franchisor, and if the franchisor's standard contract substantially fails to meet his requirements then he may be better advised to consider a different franchise operation. A franchise contract is usually a contract of adhesion and is not open to negotiation to any significant extent.

To repeat what has already been said, it is absolutely essential that the prospective franchisee seeks proper legal advice before committing himself to any agreement whatsoever. No reputable franchisor will try to pressurize a potential franchisee into signing anything before he has had the opportunity to consult a solicitor. Any franchisor who does so should be avoided at all costs.

Checklist

The more important points which should be covered in a franchise contract are:

- a description of the franchise including the granting of rights to use the franchisor's intellectual property
- the franchisee's territorial rights
- the initial and continuing fees the franchisee has to pay
- the obligations of the franchisor
- the obligations of the franchisee
- the termination of the contract by either side
- the franchisee's right to assign the business including the procedure in the event of death or incapacity of the franchisee.

10

11 A checklist for the prospective franchisee

For most franchisees, the decision to purchase a franchise represents a substantial personal and financial commitment and may well prove to be one of the most important 'career moves' that they ever make. It is therefore essential that the prospective franchisee is fully aware of exactly what it is that he is committing himself to, and what he should expect in return for that commitment. Misunderstandings and ambiguities that are not sorted out before the franchise agreement is signed can quickly develop into problems which may subsequently prove to be very difficult and costly to resolve. There can surely be no worse feeling than knowing that such a problem could have been foreseen and avoided if only the franchisee had asked sufficient questions before entering into the franchise agreement. Buying a franchise is not like taking a job as an employee – the franchisee cannot just walk away from his franchise in the way that an employee can leave his job should it fail to match up to his expectations.

Clearly the golden rule must be that the franchisee should find out as much as he possibly can about the franchisor and his operation before entering into any agreement. He should not be embarrassed to ask as many questions as are necessary in order to build up a complete picture of the franchise operation under consideration. No genuine franchisor should have any objections to answering these questions – after all, if he himself is concerned about the long-term success of his operation, then it is just as much in his interests as it is in the franchisee's to ensure that both parties are fully aware of what is involved in the relationship so that subsequent problems can be avoided.

If the franchisee makes sure that he knows the answers to the questions set out below, then he will at least be armed with some of the basic information which he ought to have before reaching a decision whether or not to go ahead with the purchase of the franchise under consideration. A checklist such as this can prove to be a very useful aid to decision making, but it is important that prospective franchisees appreciate that no two franchise operations are identical and each one must therefore be approached in a slightly different way. The questions that are included in the following checklist are, of necessity, fairly general in nature. Furthermore, this list is not intended to be exhaustive – it should be used merely as a starting point for the prospective franchisee when seeking information. So long as this point is borne in mind than the following checklist should prove to be a useful 'aide-mémoire' for the franchisee in evaluating a franchise. However, the inherent limitations of any general checklist should at all times be recognized and a degree of flexibility should be applied when drawing conclusions from the responses that are solicited. It would be unreasonable to expect that the franchisor will provide the hoped-for responses to each and every question. (Indeed it might even be considered somewhat suspect if he did.) Therefore the implications of the answers which are given in response to individual questions must be evaluated both in the light of other responses and in terms of the overall impression of the operation.

Hopefully, by talking to as many people as possible, including the franchisor, professional advisers such as lawyers and accountants, the British Franchise Association, and existing franchisees (who will often prove to be one of the most valuable sources of frank advice and information), the prospective franchisee will enter into an agreement with his eyes wide open, and the risk that the franchise may fail to live up to his expectations should be reduced. Conversely, he may become aware of the failings of the operation in time, before he signs a contract.

Checklist for the prospective franchisee

Your own motivation

- Do you have the capacity, desire and temperament to run your own business?
- Do you have special interests, skills and aptitudes?
- Are you able and prepared to work hard for long, unsocial hours?
- Can you live with the burden of borrowed money if you have to?
- Are you prepared to co-operate and work within the disciplines of the franchise?
- Do you mix well with people?
- Do you have the support of your family?

The product, service or concept

- Is it a 'fad' – or will demand be sustained?
- Is it distinctive, unique, and have a good reputation? Is it difficult to duplicate by others?
- Has it been proven by at least one successful pilot operation in a typical location over at least one year?
- How good is the competition? How do prices compare?

11

- What is the source of supply of stock, etc? Are you allowed to choose your own sources if necessary?
- Is there strong public awareness and acceptance – or will it need a lot of advertising?
- Are there patent and trade mark protections? For how long?
- Why is the owner franchising instead of using other methods of marketing?

The franchise and the franchisor

- How experienced is the franchisor? What is the track record of the franchise? Is there steady growth?
- Is the franchisor financially sound? Can you check from recent accounts or a banker's status report?
- Is any deposit paid to the franchisor refundable and if so under what circumstances?
- Is the franchisor a member of the BFA?
- Does the franchisor have enough experience within the organization to provide ongoing support?
- Is there sufficient advertising? Does the franchisor contribute?
- Is training provided, initially and later? Who pays? How much training is there?
- Is there a uniform performance monitoring system? What are the arrangements for providing field support?
- How many outlets are there? How many are company-owned?
- What are the development plans for the next five years?
- How are franchisees selected?
- How many failures have there been? Details?
- Contact existing franchisees of your own choice. Ask:

    1. How did actual cost of investment compare with the cost advertised?
    2. How accurate were profit/loss/cashflow estimates?
    3. How good was initial and subsequent support?
    4. What is franchisor like to work with? Accessible? Fair? Organized? Responsive?

Financial implications

- What is initial cost? How much is franchise fee? It should represent defrayal of the franchisor's costs without a sizable profit element.
- Will you need funds while training or until business begins to pay?
- Are financial projections realistic? How have they been arrived at? Do they take account of rent reviews? (These can be considerable.)

- Is projected income enough for you to live on and provide profit for growth? Also to pay for any borrowing, i.e. interest and capital repayments and depreciation costs.
- How does the franchisor make his money? Does he take a profit from more than one source? If you pay a management services fee (most common) is it pitched at a reasonable level?
- Can franchisor's income support the level of service you need or have been promised?
- Is there a minimum management services fee or a minimum purchase of goods requirement?

In your contract

- Is the contract fair to both parties?
- Has an exclusive territory been granted?
- What is the term of the contract? Is it renewable without onerous conditions and without a further fee?
- What provisions are there for the continuation of the business if you are incapacitated or die?
- Are obligations of both parties clearly defined?
- Under what circumstances can the contract be terminated by you/by the franchisor?
- Is there a minimum turnover clause?
- Can you sell or assign the business? Under what conditions? Are terms negotiable? They should not be. The contract should be the same for all franchisees.

11

12 Guidelines for the prospective franchisor

The decision to begin franchising □ Identifying and developing a business suitable for franchising □ Testing through pilot outlets □ The operating manual □ Head-office staff requirements □ Training programme □ Attracting prospective franchisees □ Selecting prospective franchisees □ Operating the franchise system □ Checklist

The objective of this chapter is to highlight some of the points that the prospective franchisor should bear in mind when planning and developing his proposed franchise operation. Clearly it would be unrealistic to suggest that a comprehensive guideline which would adequately cover all of the areas relating to the development of franchise operation could be presented within a single chapter (or even a whole book). This chapter will attempt to outline only some of the more basic considerations, many of which have been discussed in previous chapters. The reader would be well-advised at this stage to refer back to Chapter 3 (Essential features to look for in a business format franchise) and the points made there should be borne in mind when reading this chapter.

The decision to begin franchising

In broad terms, the decision to set up a franchise operation will usually arise out of one of three possible situations:

(a) The prospective franchisor is currently operating a successful, established business which he now wishes to expand. For some specific reason franchising appeals to him as a method of achieving this expansion (for example, he may only have limited capital and might therefore find it difficult to finance an expansion programme himself).

(b) The prospective franchisor has developed a specific product and now wishes to quickly establish an extensive distribution network for that product.

(c) The prospective franchisor has specifically set out to develop a business concept that he will be able to franchise. Thus, whereas in the first two cases franchising is merely a means to an end, i.e. the expansion of an existing business, or the distribution of a specific product, in this last case franchising is an end in itself.

In practice the first two cases occur much more frequently than the third. It is fairly uncommon to start from scratch with the franchising concept itself as the primary business objective and then try to develop a franchisable business.

Identifying and developing a business suitable for franchising

There are several characteristics which tend to be important elements in many of the most successful franchise operations:

- standardization – in the products/services, the way they are sold, and the overall image and appearance of the franchised outlets
- a distinctive business with a unique selling point
- straightforward operating methods
- suitable franchisees.

Standardization

Standardization is essential in maintaining the goodwill associated with the franchise chain. Consequently the prospective franchisor must develop a business concept which can easily be reproduced in any location. He must therefore ensure that any equipment which is essential to the operation of the franchise will be readily available at a reasonable price. Similarly, when designing the interior of the franchises, the colour scheme and décor that is chosen must be easily reproducible in different locations over time.

Distinctive business

12

The business must be distinctive and noticeable in order to distinguish it from its competitors. It should have some sort of unique selling point which cannot easily be copied by others. Trade marks and service marks should be used to protect business names, logos etc., wherever possible.

Operating methods

The operating methods which are involved in the business must be reasonably straightforward so that franchisees can quickly learn the operating system. Prospective franchisees cannot afford to spend months learning the system – they must be able to develop the required skills within, say, a couple of weeks so that they can open their outlet and have it operational as soon as possible.

Franchisees

The franchisor should identify exactly what sort of characteristics he is looking for in a franchisee and he must be sure that he will be able to attract an adequate supply of suitable people with the required personal characteristics and financial resources. Similarly there must be a ready supply of suitable staff to work for the franchisees.

Outlet location

The requirements of the proposed operation in terms of the location of outlets must also be ascertained. The franchisor must calculate the required daily pedestrian/vehicular traffic flow that is required in order to make a location viable. Other considerations include the requirements for nearby parking, the type of road that would be suitable, etc. For example, a dual carriageway might have a very high traffic flow but passing cars may be unable to stop at the outlet because of the speed at which the traffic is moving, or because of parking restrictions. Furthermore, on this type of road the traffic using the opposite carriageway should not necessarily be considered as potential passing trade, especially if there is a central reservation or barrier separating the two sides of the road. Certain types of business will benefit greatly from being located near to a landmark or an entertainment facility. For example, a fast-food restaurant will enjoy the additional trade that is generated by people using a nearby cinema or sports complex. Having defined the 'ideal' location the franchisor must determine whether such outlets will be readily available at a price that the franchisees will be able to afford. The franchisees will often expect the franchisor to assist them in selecting a suitable site for their outlet, so if possible he should try to develop some sort of relationship with commercial estate agents in each area in which he intends to franchise outlets. For a non-retail franchise the location may be less important than, say, the use of an established telephone number, for example, in the case of a take-away food franchise. If this is the case then the franchise contract should clearly stipulate that upon termination of the agreement the telephone number will revert to the franchisor, so that the ex-franchisee cannot set up his own business using the established telephone number, thereby 'poaching' the franchisor's trade.

Financial forecasts

Before selling any franchises the prospective franchisor must make projections of the turnover, costs, profit, and cash-flow which the 'typical' franchised outlet should expect to be able to generate. The assistance of a good accountant will prove invaluable in preparing these forecasts, bearing in mind that tax considerations must be taken account of in preparing profit and cash-flow forecasts. It is of course essential that all forecasts should be based on realistic assumptions. The projections are likely to enjoy greater credibility if the most important assumptions are made explicit. Three sets of projections could be made: one based on 'pessimistic' assumptions, one based on 'optimistic' assumptions, and one based on 'most likely' assumptions. The probability of each of these three outcomes actually occurring should also be estimated. By multiplying each outcome by its corresponding probability and then adding together the three resulting figures, the franchisor may derive the 'expected value' of turnover, costs, profit etc. This figure represents the 'average' results that might be expected.

Each franchise must be capable of generating sufficient profit to enable both the franchisee and the franchisor to earn an adequate return on their respective investments. Consequently a business which generates a high gross margin or a very high turnover is desirable.

'Value added'

A high 'value added' content is always a desirable feature in a franchise. Value added can be defined as the increase in realizable value of a product or service resulting from an alteration in the form, location, or availability of that product or service. In other words the franchisee should actually 'do' something to the inputs to his operation in order to transform them into the finished product, rather than simply reselling bought-in products in their original form without changing them in any way. For example, a franchisee in a fast-food operation will usually buy in the necessary ingredients, which he then mixes and cooks in order to make the final product. A high value added should not only result in a greater gross margin on sales, but also, as a general rule, the higher the value added, the easier it is for the franchisee to differentiate the products that he sells from those of a competitor, since the franchisee himself plays a greater role in transforming the inputs into the final product and he therefore has more opportunity to make the final product different in some way.

Target market

The franchisor must identify the target market that the proposed franchise is intended to serve. This will usually be a specific segment of a wider market. For example, if the franchise is to be a cleaning operation, is it aimed primarily at domestic households or commercial properties and offices? The market for each may be quite different. Once a specific market segment has been identified the franchisor should determine the market size (in terms of both volume and value) and growth rate. He must have a clear objective as to what market share he intends to capture within a specified time period. He must also have a realistic plan stating how he intends to capture this market share from established competitors already operating in the market. The franchisor may intend to compete on the basis of price, quality, speed of service, etc., but he must be sure that whatever it is he can offer will be sufficient to attract customers away from their usual source of supply. Established customer loyalty can often be extremely difficult to overcome.

Is franchising the best method of expansion?

Having developed the business concept the franchisor must be absolutely convinced not only that he has a franchisable business proposition, but also that franchising is the optimal method of expansion. He should once again review all the alternatives before deciding that franchising is indeed the best route to follow. The franchisor will find that it is extremely difficult to extricate himself from the franchise system once he has sold franchised outlets. He must recognize that he has a continuing obligation (moral as well as contractual) to the franchisees who have made a substantial personal investment in their businesses, and he must therefore approach franchising as a long-term commitment.

Capital

Another extremely important point to note is that although a franchisor can achieve expansion by utilizing the capital of franchisees the setting up and developing of a franchise operation still demands a sizeable outlay on his part. The franchisor's initial investment could be anything up to a quarter of a million pounds if he wishes to develop a national network. He will probably take at least three years before the operation manages to break even. The franchisor must ensure that he has adequate working capital to survive the first few years until the revenues begin to flow. Fortunately, he can recoup these costs as the network develops.

Testing through pilot outlets

If the franchisor decides to go ahead with his plans to franchise his operation, then it is essential that the business concept is fully developed before the first franchise is sold. It is unethical to use the franchisees as guinea-pigs, and their business will soon suffer if operating methods are constantly having to be changed simply because the system was not fully thought out and tested before being sold as a franchise. Therefore at least one, and preferably several, franchisor-owned pilot outlets should be set up. These outlets should be operated for at least one year in order to rigorously test the proposed franchise operation under actual working conditions. A period of less than twelve months will be insufficient to highlight the extent of any seasonal fluctuations in sales. The pilot outlets should be run using exactly the same operating methods as the franchisees will be required to use. This process will not only demonstrate whether there is a continuing demand for the product or service, but will also reveal whether the proposed operating systems are effective. All shortcomings in the system should be corrected and retested in the pilot outlet until the franchise operation has been refined and perfected. It is essential that the pilot outlet is set up in a typical location, otherwise it will not be representative of the conditions under which the average franchisee will have to operate.

The financial results achieved in the pilot outlets should be used to re-assess whether the franchisor's original projections were realistic. It may be necessary to adjust the original figures (either upwards or downwards) in the light of any variance between the forecasts and the actual results achieved in the pilot outlets. When presented with a set of profit forecasts for a proposed outlet, a franchisee (or his accountant) will usually ask for supporting evidence to demonstrate that these figures are indeed realistic. The franchisor can use the results from the pilot operation to justify his projected figures.

The operating manual

The experience gained through operating the pilot outlets can be used as a basis for compiling an operating manual. This is effectively the franchisee's 'bible'. It gives detailed explanations of all the operating systems that the franchisee is required to employ, and it is in effect a blue print for the operation of the franchise. The franchisor should find that it is well worth while investing sufficient time and effort in compiling the operating manual to ensure that it is comprehensive and easily understandable. The franchisee will then be able to solve many of the day-to-day operational problems that he will encounter by referring to the manual rather than having constantly to contact the franchisor for advice and assistance. Consequently the franchisor's head-office staff will be free to concentrate on the management and efficient operation of the overall chain rather than having to deal with relatively trivial operating problems of individual franchisees.

Head-office staff requirements

While the franchisor is initially developing his business idea he may be able to rely on staff who are already in his employment. It is, however, important for him to recognize that once he sets out on the actual franchising programme he will inevitably have to face up to hiring additional staff in order to ensure that the operation continues to run efficiently. In the past, many would-be franchisors have attempted to set up opertions on a shoestring and have resisted taking on the necessary personnel. The result is almost invariably a patently ineffective and unconvincing operation. Prospective franchisees will quickly be put off if it is obvious to them that the franchisor does not have the resources that would be required in order to provide adequate head-office support for the franchisees. The franchisor will eventually have to take on additional specialist staff who have the skills to train new franchisees and help them with any routine operational difficulties. He may also decide to recruit a franchise sales manager. The franchisor may be all in favour of performance-related salaries for his employees, but there is a strong case for arguing that the sales manager should not be paid on the basis of how many franchises he manages to sell, otherwise the temptation to recruit unsuitable franchisees in order to boost his salary may be too great to resist. After all, the sales manager is not committing himself to any long-term relationship with the franchisees.

As has been stated elsewhere in this text, the franchisor must accept that he is no longer simply in the business of selling a particular product. He is now primarily in the business of setting others up to sell that product. The franchisor must therefore develop different skills from those that he originally required, and he must also be prepared to hire new personnel who possess those skills that the franchisor himself lacks and which are called for in the operation of the franchise chain.

Training programme

Franchisees must be provided with comprehensive training in the basic operating methods before they can commence trading in their own outlet. The franchisor must therefore develop an adequate educational programme which will usually consist of a combination of both classroom teaching and practical experience gained by working either in the franchisor-owned outlets, or in an existing franchised unit. In most cases the franchisor-owned outlets will represent the best source of practical experience since existing franchisees will naturally be more concerned with getting on with the day-to-day operation of their own outlet rather than with trying to train a newcomer. Furthermore, there is a danger that an established franchisee will pass on his bad habits to a new recruit. The franchisor can exercise greater control over the content of the practical training which is received by the franchisee if that training is provided in a franchisor-owned outlet.

The training period is extremely important as it is during this time that the basis of the relationship between the franchisee and the franchisor will be formed, and an effective educational programme will instill the franchisee's confidence in the franchisor.

Attracting prospective franchisees

Once the franchise package has been fully developed and a franchise contract has been drawn up with the help of a specialist solicitor, the franchisor is then ready to start selling his first outlets. He must therefore decide how he intends to market the franchise package. In order to be able to advertise in the press the franchisor must first apply to Newspaper Publishers Association Ltd (6 Bouverie Street, London EC4Y Tel: 01 583 8132) for permission to advertise. Many national newspapers have special business sections (the *Sunday Times* often includes a special franchise section in its classified adverts). There is also a specialist trade publication in the form of *Franchise World Magazine*.

Many franchisors rely heavily on favourable editorial comment about the operation rather than on direct advertising copy. This serves a dual purpose in that it not only promotes existing outlets but also generates interest from prospective franchisees at the same time. With this in mind many franchisors organize special launches for new outlets and also arrange regular promotional activities on both a local and a national basis. The press is regularly attracted by the 'employee turned successful businessman' type of story which can be written about franchisees!

Trade shows are becoming an increasingly important marketing opportunity and the BFA-backed Franchise Exhibitions have become the focal point of many franchisors' marketing programmes. The national press invariably carry many stories and features on franchising around the time of the Exhibitions and this helps to increase the effectiveness of concurrent marketing campaigns.

Membership of the British Franchise Association is an invaluable aid in

12

marketing a franchise operation not only because of the publicity the Association generates for its member companies, but also because membership is seen as being an indication that the franchisor is an 'ethical' operator.

It is important that in marketing his operation the franchisor resists the temptation to use the 'hard-sell', particularly in the early days when he may be over-anxious to make his first sales. The danger of this approach is that in his enthusiasm to secure a sale he may, either accidentally or deliberately, make misrepresentations about the potential of an outlet to a prospective franchisee. This will inevitably result in problems, or possibly even legal action, at a later date.

Selecting prospective franchisees

The somewhat unique nature of the franchise relationship means that the franchisor must be extremely careful when selecting prospective franchisees. This is a point which has been discussed at various points in preceding chapters. Basically the franchisor should avoid individuals who would be likely to resent the continuing control that the franchisor must exercise over them. He must look for more in a franchisee than simply the ability to provide the required financial investment. Every prospective franchisee will have his own individual strengths and weaknesses and must therefore be judged on an individual basis. However, it may prove useful for the franchisor to draw up some sort of 'ideal franchisee profile' against which applicants can be compared. This should cover aspects such as:

- financial resources required
- previous business/employment experience
- personality
- pychological make-up
- marital status
- age
- health.

This 'ideal' profile can be used as a useful screening device when evaluating applicants. The exact requirements will vary from one franchise to the next, but the whole success of any franchise chain hinges upon careful selection of franchisees.

The franchisor should avoid the temptation to offer any special deals simply in order to get the initial franchises sold. Before he begins marketing the franchise he should have already determined the appropriate level at which to set initial fees, continuing management services fees, etc., and he should have drawn up a standard franchise contract. It is important that all franchisees are offered exactly the same deal. In effect this means that the franchise agreement must be a contract of adhesion, i.e. a 'take it or leave it' contract, somewhat like an insurance policy, rather than a negotiated agreement. A few prospective franchisees may be put off by what appears to them to be simply stubbornness on the part of the franchisor, but inconsistencies in the terms offered to different individuals are likely to cause resentment and discontent amongst the franchisees at a later stage. It is not surprising that having spent a lot of time, effort, and money in developing his franchise package, the franchisor will be extremely keen to secure the sale of the first few outlets, but many franchisors have regretted offering special terms in their eagerness to recruit franchisees.

Operating the franchise system

The franchisor must maintain close contact with the franchisees in order to ensure a high degree of two-way communication between the two parties. This will go a long way towards preventing dissatisfaction developing among franchisees as it will allow them the opportunity to air any grievances that they may have. The franchisor should also avoid using coercive sources of power, such as using the threat of termination of the franchise contract as a means of controlling the franchisee. This has been shown to be a cause of dissatisfaction amongst franchisees. The franchisor should always try to use persuasive tactics rather than being seen to be trying to impose his contractual right of control over the franchisee. Having said that, the franchisor must ensure standardization at all costs. He must therefore make certain that the franchisees do not deviate from any of the recommended operating methods as outlined in the operating manual, and he must take swift corrective action at the first signs of any such deviation. Standardization is the key element in developing and maintaining customer loyalty and goodwill.

12

Advance planning

The above points can represent no more than a mere handful of the more important considerations which must be borne in mind by anyone who is contemplating setting up a franchise chain. The relative importance of each of these points, and of others not included above, will vary from one operation to the next. However, the one thing which is crucial to the success of every franchise operation is thorough advance planning. The franchisor must have fully developed his business concept before he starts franchising. That is not to say that he should not introduce improvements whenever possible, or that changes will not be needed over time in order to keep the franchise contemporary, but he should not be seen to be using the first few franchises as experiments. He must instill in the franchisees absolute confidence that his business concept is sound and that his operating systems are effective. After all, that is what they are paying for when they buy a franchise. The franchisor must therefore anticipate and be fully prepared for any situation which may arise. If the franchisees feel that the franchisor is in any way unprepared then they are likely to lose faith in his ability to oversee the operation of their outlets. Since the franchise relationship is based on mutual trust and confidence, the system will soon collapse if the franchisees suspect that the franchisor is not totally in control.

Checklist

1. Successful franchises are characterized by:
   - standard products and image
   - a unique selling point
   - simple operating methods
   - suitable franchisees.
2. In determining whether or not the business is suitable for franchising the franchisor must:
   - define the 'ideal' location for outlets
   - identify the target market
   - construct profit, breakeven and cashflow forecasts for a typical outlet
   - ensure that he has sufficient capital to establish the franchise.
3. The franchisor must then:
   - test the operation through pilot schemes
   - compile the operating manual
   - ensure that he has the head-office staff to provide support for franchisees
   - set up a comprehensive training programme
   - attract and select franchisees.

Appendix:
Useful addresses – list of
British Franchise
Association members and
associates

The following list of addresses represents the British Franchise Association's membership as at December 1988.

Further information can be obtained direct from the BFA, who publish a Franchise Information Book for prospective franchisees. The BFA's address is: British Franchise Association, Franchise Chambers, Thames View, Newtown Road, Henley-on-Thames, Oxon RG9 1HG, Tel: (0491) 578049.

British Franchise Association full members' list (December 1988)

Franchisors are required to submit a completed application form, including disclosure document, franchise agreement, prospectus, accounts, etc., and provide proof of a correctly constituted pilot scheme successfully operated for at least one year, financed and managed by the applicant company. In addition, evidence of successful franchising over a subsequent two-year period with at least four franchisees is required.

ACCOUNTING CENTRE (THE) Elscot House Arcadia Avenue London N3 2JE	Mr I. Davies 01-349 3191	Computerized accounting services and company 'doctor' service
ALAN PAUL HAIRDRESSING PLC 164 New Chester Road Birkenhead Merseyside	Mr M. Rowland 051 666 1060	Ladies' and gentlemen's hairdressing and retail

**ALFRED MARKS
(FRANCHISE) LTD**
Adia House
84–86 Regent Street
London W1A 1AL

Mr M. Horgan
01 437 7855

Employment bureau

**ALPINE SOFT
DRINKS PLC**
Richmond Way
Chelmsley Wood
Birmingham B37 7TT

Mr J. Flanagan
021 770 6816

Sales of soft drinks and
allied products direct to
consumers at their homes

ANC HOLDINGS LTD
Berryhill Trading Estate
Victoria Road
Fenton
Stoke-on-Trent
Staffs ST4 2NS

Mr D.L. Boon
0782 712221

Next-day nationwide
parcel freight delivery/
collection service

**ANICARE GROUP
SERVICES
(VETERINARY)
LTD**
27 Buckingham Road
Shoreham-by-Sea
Sussex BN4 5UA

Mr J.P. Sheridan
0273 463022

Management services to
the veterinary profession

A P AUTELA
Regal House
Birmingham Road
Stratford upon Avon
Warks CV37 0BN

Mr R. Raylor
0789 414545

Automotive part suppliers

**APOLLO WINDOW
BLINDS LTD**
79 Johnstone Avenue
Cardonald Industrial
Estate
Glasgow G52 4YH

Mr J. Watson
041 810 3021

Manufacturers and
retailers of window blinds
to the domestic and
commercial markets

**AVIS RENT A CAR
LTD**
Trident House
Station Road
Hayes
Middx UB3 4DJ

Mr M. McInerney
01 848 8765

Short-term car rental

BADGEMAN LTD **SKETCHLEY** **BUSINESS SERVICE** **GROUP** 544 High Road Chiswick London W4 5RG	Mr T.A. Howarth 01 994 0826	Manufacture and sale of personalized name badges
BALLY GROUP (UK) **LTD** Wells House 79 Wells Street London W1P 4JL	Mr P.W. Peters 01 631 4222	Retail shoes
BALMFORTH & **PARTNERS** **(FRANCHISES)** St. Mary's House Duke Street Norwich NR3 1QA	Mr A.R. Balmforth 0603 660555	Residential estate agency
BODY AND FACE **PLACE** 164 New Chester Road Birkenhead Merseyside	Mr H. Miller 051 666 1060	Retail natural health and skincare products
BRITANNIA **BUSINESS SALES LTD** Britannia Buildings Park Gate Bradford W. Yorks BD1 5BS	Mr J.G. Thompson 0274 722977	Licensed trade specialists
BRITISH DAMP **PROOFING** The School House Fleetwood Road Esprick Preston PR4 3HJ	Mr A. Haslam 039 136 441	Damp proofing/timber treatment
BUDGET RENT-A- **CAR** **INTERNATIONAL** **INC** 41 Marlowes Hemel Hempstead Herts HP1 1LD	Mr N. Summerville 0442 232555	National and international self-drive car, van and truck rental service

Appx

BURGERKING (UK) LTD 20 Kew Road Richmond Surrey TW9 2NA	Mr J. Scott 01 940 6046	Fast food restaurants
CIRCLE C STORES LTD 24 Fitzalan Road Foffey Horsham W. Sussex RH13 6AA	Mr J. Wormull 0403 210450	Convenience stores
CIRCLE K (UK) LTD Fareham Point Wickham Road Fareham Hants PO16 7BU	Mr J.R. Hunt 0329 822666	Convenience stores
CITY LINK TRANSPORT HOLDINGS LTD Batavia Road Sunbury on Thames Middx TW16 5LR	Mr R. Thomas 0932 788799	Same day and overnight parcel delivery service.
CLARKS SHOES LTD 40 High Street Street Somerset BA16 0YA	Mr P. Monaghan 0458 43131	Retail shoe shops
COCA COLA EXPORT CORPORATION (THE) *(Please note: no further franchises are available)*	Mr D. Rodin	Soft drinks. Contact the BFA direct for addresses of northern and southern bottlers
COLOUR COUNSELLORS LTD 187 New King's Road Parsons Green London SW6	Mrs V. Stourton 01 736 8326	Interior decorating. Colour catalogued samples of wallpapers, carpets and fabrics

COMMAND PERFORMANCE INT. LTD 256 High Street Slough Berks SL1 1JU	Mr J.G. Macaulay (0753) 822645	Ladies' and men's hairdressing and beauty
COMPUTERLAND EUROPE SARL 518 Elder House Elder Gate Central Milton Keynes Bucks	Mr C. Booth Mr S. Evans 0908 664244	Retail sale of micromcomputer software and hardware
COUNTRY ROSE MANAGEMENT (FRANCHISE) LTD Country Properties 41 High Street Baldock Herts SG7 5NP	Mr N.J. Ramsden 0462 896148	Full estate agency service specializing in country towns, villages and rural areas
CROWN EYEGLASS PLC Glenfield Park Northrop Avenue Blackburn Lancs BB1 5QF	Mr J. Lee 0254 51535	Sale of prescription spectacles
DAMPCURE/ WOODCURE 30 Darley House Cow Lane Garston Watford Herts	Mr B. Roberts 0923 663322	Damp proofing/timber treatment
DON MILLER'S HOT BREAD KITCHENS 166 Bute Street Mall Arndale Centre Luton Beds LU1 2TL	Mr M.J.B. Ward 0582 422781	Hot bread kitchens

Appx

DYNO-SERVICES LTD Zockoll House 143 Maple Road Surbiton Surrey KT6 4BJ	Mr Peter Williams 01 549 9711	Drain and pipe cleaning service
EUROCLEAN 13 The Office Village 4 Romford Road London E15 4BZ	Mr J. Hopkinson 01 519 3045	Dry cleaning
EVERETT MASSON & FURBY LTD 18 Walsworth Road Hitchin Herts SG4 9SP	Mr A. Madden FNAEA 0462 32377	Business and commercial property agents
EXCHANGE TRAVEL (FRANCHISES) LTD Exchange House 66/70 Parker Road Hastings E. Sussex TN34 3UB	Mr D. Beechinor Hastings (0424) 423571 Ext. 206	Travel agency
FASTFRAME FRANCHISES LTD 28 Blandford Street Sunderland SR1 3JH	Mr Ian Johnson 091 565 2233	Instant picture and related framing service
FERSINA INTERNATIONAL Cestrum House Industry Road Carlton Industrial Estate Carlton Barnsley S. Yorks S70 3NH	Mr Paul S. Hinchliffe 0226 728310	Sale, manufacture and installation of uPVC conservatories, doors and windows
FRANCESCO GROUP Woodings Yard Bailey Street Stafford ST17 4BG	Mr F. Dellicompagni 0785 47175	Ladies' and gents' hairdressing

GLOBAL CLEANING CONTRACTS LTD 8–10 High Street Sutton Surrey SM1 1HN	Mr K. Wearn 01 642 0054	Office cleaning, contract sales and management agency
GREAT ADVENTURE GAME (THE) Bergen Mews 158a Blythe Road Hammersmith London W14 0HL	Mr J. Wright 01 940 7644	Outdoor tactical adventure game for adults held in woodlands
GUN-POINT LTD Thavies Inn House 3/4 Holborn Circus London EC1N 2PL	Mr I. Ruddlesden 01 353 6167	A mechanized repointing service for all brick and stone properties
HOLIDAY INNS (UK) LTD 62 London Road Staines Middx TW18 4HB	Mr P.M. Gee 0784 65810	Hotels
HOLLAND AND BARRETT FRANCHISING LTD Canada Road Byfleet Surrey KT14 7JL	Mr K. Mullarkey 09323 36022	Health food retail stores
HOME TUNE LTD 77 Mount Ephraim Tunbridge Wells Kent TN4 8BS	Mr R. Deslandes 0892 510532	Car tuning service
INTERLINK EXPRESS PARCELS LTD Portland House 22/24 Portland Square Bristol BS2 8RZ	Mr R. Gabriel Bristol (0272) 426900	Express courier parcel service
IN-TOTO LTD Wakefield Road Gildersome Leeds LS27 0QW	Mr M. Eccleston Leeds (0532) 524131	Retailing of kitchens and bathroom furniture, appliances and ancillary merchandise

Appx

KALL-KWIK PRINTING (UK) LTD
Kall-Kwik House
106 Pembroke Road
Ruislip
Middx HA4 8NW

Mr M. Gerstenhaber
08956 32700

Quick printing centres offering comprehensive design, printing, finishing and photocopying service

KEITH HALL HAIRDRESSING
119–121 Derby Road
Long Eaton
Nottingham NG10 4LA

Mr R.B. Gosnell
0602 729914

Ladies' and gents' hairdressing

KENTUCKY FRIED CHICKEN (GB) LTD
Wicat House
403 London Road
Camberley
Surrey GU15 3HL

Mr P. Whittle
Camberley 0276 686151

Fast food

KNOBS & KNOCKERS FRANCHISING LTD
Hathaway House
7d Woodfield Road
London W9 2EA

Mr J.R. Staddon
01 289 4764

The sale, using retail shop premises, of internal and external door furniture, in brass, black iron and porcelain, together with co-ordinating brass light switches, dimmers and sockets, etc.

KWIK STRIP (UK) LTD
Units 1/2
The 306 Estate
242 Broomhill Road
Brislington
Bristol BS4 5RA

Mr I. Chivers
0272 772470

Service to trade and retail markets for the stripping and restoration of furniture

THE LATE LATE SUPERSHOP (UK) LTD
PO Box 53
New Century House
Manchester M60 4ES

Mr J.M. Campbell
061 834 1212

Convenience store retailing

MASTER THATCHERS LTD Rose Tree Farm 29 Nine Mile Ride Finchampstead Wokingham Berks RG11 4QD	Mr R.C. West 0734 734203	Thatching in water reed and combed wheat reed including repairs, patching and re-ridging
METRO-ROD PLC Metro House Churchill Way Macclesfield Ches SK11 6AY	Mr J.L.B. Harris 0625 34444	Domestic and industrial drain and pipe cleaning and allied work
MIDAS (GREAT BRITAIN) LTD 107 Mortlake High Street London SW14 8HH	Mr Phillips 01 878 7803	Retail exhaust system replacement
MIXAMATE HOLDINGS LTD Station Yard Bourne Way Hayes Kent BR2 7EY	Mr P. Bates 01 462 8011	Specialized concrete delivery service to builders and DIY
MOBILETUNING LTD 7a Nelson Road Greenwich London SE10 9JB	Mr A.R. Rowntree 01 853 1520	Mobile car engine-tuning service
MOLLY MAID UK Hamilton Road Slough Berks	Mr M. Tall 0753 23388/35343	Domestic cleaning service
NATIONWIDE INVESTIGATIONS 86 Southwark Bridge Road London SE1 OEX	Mr K. Walker 01 928 1799	Private investigations bureau

Appx

NORTHERN DAIRIES LTD 3 Balne Lane Wakefield WF2 0DL	Mr D. Broomhead (Distribution Development Manager) 0924 290660	The manufacture, processing, packaging, marketing and distribution of milk and diary produce
OASIS TRADING Oasis Park Eynsham Oxford OX8 1TR	Mr M. Bennet 0865 882888	Retail of clothing, jewellery, accessories, etc.
OLIVERS (UK) LTD Eagle Court Harpur Street Bedford MK40 1JZ	Mr N.H. Allen 0234 328181	Bakery and coffee shops
PDC COPYPRINT (FRANCHISE) LTD 1 Church Lane East Grinstead W. Sussex RH19 3AZ	Mr M. Marks 0342 315321	Quick printing shops
PANCAKE PLACE LTD (THE) Clydesdale Bank House 30 New Road Milnathort Kinross KY13 7XT	Mr R.D. Kay Kinross (0577) 63969	Pancake restaurants
PASS & CO Passco House 635 High Road Leytonstone London E11 4RD	Mr Allen Winter 01 539 1105	Timber preservation
PERFECT PIZZA (THE) Pizza Restaurants 65 Staines Road Hounslow Middx TW3 3HW	Mr M. Clayton 01 570 2323	Restaurants and take away units
PIP (UK) LTD Black Arrow House 2 Chandos Road London NW10 6NF	Mr C. Graham 01 965 0700	Photocopying, instant printing, artwork and graphic communications

PIZZA EXPRESS LTD 29 Wardour Street London W1V 3HB	Mr J. Dell 01 437 7215	Pizzeria restaurants
POPPIES (UK) LTD 31 Houndgate Darlington Co Durham	Mrs S. Rorstad 0325 488699	Domestic and commercial cleaning
PRACTICAL USED CAR RENTAL LTD 137/145 High Street Bordesley Birmingham B12 0JU	Mr B. Agnew 021 771 4524	Practical used car rental
PRONTAPRINT PLC Coniscliffe House Darlington Co Durham DL3 7EX	Mr P. Stanton 0325 483333	Fast print centres incorporating artwork and design, commercial copying and business communications services
PRONUPTIA- YOUNGS LTD 70–78 York Way King's Cross London N1 9AG	Mrs L. Ivinson 01 278 0343	Bridal attire retail shops. Formal wear hire service for men
RODIER PARIS Station House 81–83 Fulham High Street London SW6 3JW	Mrs R. Green 01 731 7390	Fully co-ordinated range of ladies' and gentlemens' fashion clothing
SAKS HAIR (HOLDINGS) LTD 57 Coniscliffe Road Darlington Co Durham DL3 7EH	Mr D. Cheesebrough 0325 380333	Ladies' and gents' hairdressing
SAFECLEAN INTERNATIONAL (D.G. Cook Ltd) Delmae House Home Farm Ardington Wantage Oxon OX12 8PN	Mr D. Cook 0235 833022	Hand-cleaning of carpets and upholstery. Curtain cleaning on site.

SERVICEMASTER LTD 50 Commercial Square Freeman's Common Leicester LE2 7SR	Mr R. Rouse Leicester (0533) 548620	On-site carpet, upholstery and curtain cleaning. Fire and flood restoration, carpet treatment and repairs
SILVER SHIELD SCREENS LTD Wheler Road Seven Stars Estate Whitley Coventry CV3 4LA	Mr J. Oliver Coventry (0203) 307755	24-hour mobile windscreen replacement service
SINGER SDL LTD Unit H Grafton Way West Ham Industrial Estate Basingstoke RG22 6HZ	Mr C. Burr 0256 56291	Retail and after-sales service of sewing machines and other related products
SNAP-ON-TOOLS LTD Palmer House ·150–154 Cross Street Sale Ches M33 1AQ	Mr M. Lancaster 061 969 0126	Distribution of automotive hand tools
SNIPS IN FASHION c/o Eurobe Ltd Station Approach St Mary Cray Station Orpington Kent BR5 2NB	Mr W.H. Edwards (0689) 22722	Retail sale of ladies' designer clothes
SPUD-U-LIKE LTD 34/38 Standard Road London NW10 6EU	Mr T. Schlesinger Mr M. Porripp 01 965 0182	Fast food restaurants based on baked potatoes with large variety of fillings
STRACHAN STUDIO Cross Green Way Cross Green Industrial Est Leeds LS9 ORS	Mr G. Strachan 0532 495694	Sale of fitted bedroom furniture
SWINTON INSURANCE 31/33 Princess Street Manchester M2 4EW	Mr Peter Lowe 061 236 8697	Insurance brokers

THORNTONS
J.W. Thornton Ltd
Derwent Street
Belper
Derbys DE5 1WP

Mr R.E. Smith
Belper (077 382)
4181

Specialist chocolate and
sugar confectionery

TIE RACK LTD
Capital Interchange Way
Brentford
Middx TW8 0EX

Mr R. Delnevo
01 995 1344

Retail neckware and
accessories

TNT (UK) LTD
TNT PARCEL OFFICE
TNT House
Long Street
Atherstone
Warks CV9 1VS

Mr Ken Young
0827 715311

Collection points for
guaranteed next day
delivery nationwide plus
European and
international courier
service

TRAVAIL
EMPLOYMENT
GROUP LTD
42a Cricklade Street
Cirencester
Glos

Mr C. Rogers
0285 69201

Business employment
agency

UNIGATE DAIRIES
LTD
14/40 Victoria Road
Aldershot
Hants GU1 11TH

Mr E.H. Fince
Aldershot (0252)
24522

Distribution of milk and
dairy products and soft
drinks

UTICOLOR (GREAT
BRITAIN) LTD
Sheraton House
35 North Street
York YO1 1JD

Mr E. Bottomley
York (0904) 37798

Repair, recolouring and
restoration of vinyl
coverings

WETHERBY
TRAINING SERVICES
15 Victoria Street
Wetherby
W. Yorks LS22 4RE

Mr D.G. Button
0937 63940

Secretarial and word
processing training
centres

Appx

WIMPY
INTERNATIONAL
LTD
10 Windmill Road
Chiswick
London W4 1SD

Mr M. Cook
01 994 6454

Fast food

YVES ROCHER (LONDON) LTD 664 Victoria Road South Ruislip Middx HA4 0NY	Mr B. Saunders 01 845 1222	Exclusive retail sale of Yves Rocher beauty products range plus beauty/sun treatments

---

Note from Director

It should be borne in mind that, although franchising substantially reduces the inherent risk in a new business venture, it does not automatically guarantee success.

At the same time, registration with or membership of this or any other Association does not automatically protect the member company, or his franchisee, against commercial failure.

BFA Administrative Office:
Franchise Chambers
Thames View
Newtown Road
Henley-on-Thames
Oxon RG9 1HG
(0491) 578049

British Franchise Association Register of Associates (December 1988)

Franchisors are required to submit a completed application form, including disclosure document, franchise agreement, prospectus, accounts, etc., and provide proof of a correctly constituted pilot scheme successfully operated for at least one year, financed and managed by the applicant company (as for Full Membership) but with evidence of successful franchising for a period of one year with at least one franchisee.

In addition, substantial companies with more than 25 company-owned outlets offering a franchise concept which is a replica of the existing business, with a separate franchise division, correctly constructed agreement, pilot scheme, prospectus and accounts but without a franchisee on station at the time of application, will also be eligible under this category.

A1 DAMPPROOFING New Side Mill Charnley Fold Lane Bamber Bridge Preston Lancs PR5 6AA	Mr J.B. Pickup 0772 35228	Treatment of damp and timber infestation
AUTOSHEEN CAR VALETING SERVICES (UK) LTD Unit 4 Everitt Close Denington Industrial Estate Wellingborough Northants NN8 2QE	Mr M. Shirran 0933 72347	Mobile car valeting service
BANSON TOOL HIRE Pellon Lane Halifax HX1 5SB	Mr J.P. Sharp 0422 331177	Tool hire and sles
BATH DOCTOR (THE) Denbigh House Denbigh Road Bletchley Milton Keynes MK1 1YP	Mr M.H. Robertson 0908 270007 0908 368071	Renovation of bathroom suites
BELLINA LTD 31 Knightsdale Road Ipswich IP1 4JJ	Mr K.C. Ball 0473 47444	Retail sale of Belgian chocolates
BERNI RESTAURANTS Oxford House 97 Oxford Road Uxbridge UB8 1HX	Mr D.J. Mitchell 0895 70955	Franchised licensed restaurants
BLINKERS Consort Court off High Street Fareham Hants PO16 7AL	Mr M.P. Gower 0329 230580	Ladies' and gents' hairdressing

Appx

CHICO CHIMNEY LININGS LTD Westleton Saxmundham Suffolk	Mr R.J. Hadfield 0728 73608	The re-lining of domestic and industrial chimneys
COFFEEMAN MAN-AGEMENT LTD 73 Woolsbridge Ind. Park Wimborne Dorset BH21 6SU	Mr S. Bayless 0202 823501	Selling of fresh-ground coffee, tea and machinery
COMPUTA TUNE Unit 3 Richmond Industrial Est Brown Street Accrington Lancs BB5 0RJ	Mr A. Whittaker 0254 391792/ 385891	Mobile tuning and servicing of motor cars
COUNTRYWIDE GARDEN MAINTE-NANCE SERVICES 154–200 Stockport Road Cheadle Cheshire SK8 2DP	Mr M. Stott 061 428 4444	Garden maintenance service to private houses, hotels, offices, industrial sites, etc.
CURTAIN DREAM PLC 63 Nesfield Street Bradford W. Yorks BD1 3ET	Helen James 0274 728719	Soft furnishing retailer
DASH LTD P.O. Box 5 Rowdell Road Northolt Middx UB5 5QT	Mrs J. Sebry 01 845 7777	Retailing of fashion leisure-wear
DIRECT SALON SERVICES LTD Newport Way Cannon Park Middlesbrough Cleveland TS1 5JW	Mr D. McGouran 0642 217978	Mobile van sales of hair-care and beauty products to hairdressing and beauty salons

FIRES & THINGS LTD Heat House 4 Brighton Road Horsham W. Sussex RH13 5BA	Mr M. Durrant 0403 56227	Retail of fires, fireplaces and accessories
GARDEN BUILDING CENTRES LTD Coppice Gate Lye Head Bewdley Worcs DY12 2UX	Mr I.R. Brown 0299 266361/ 266337	Sale of garden buildings, including greenhouses, summerhouses, sheds and conservatories
HOUSE OF COLOUR 1 Saint Catherine Mews Milner Street Chelsea London SW3 2PU	S.P.M. Fox-Ness 01 581 3281	Personalized colour con- sultancy and style consul- tancy with related product sales and service
M & B MARQUEES Unit 16 Swinborne Court Burnt Mills Industrial Est Basildon Essex	Mr J. Mansfield 0268 728361	Hire of marquees and ancillary equipment
MAINLY MARINES FRANCHISING LTD 6 Trojan Way Croydon Surrey CR0 4XL	Mr J. Driscoll 01 681 8421	Retail aquatic centres
MORLEY'S (FAST FOODS) LTD 162 Clapham High Street Clapham London SW4	Mr F. Moore 01 622 4821	Fast food takeaway outlets
MR LIFT LTD The Lifthouse Gloucester Road Bristol BS12 4HY	Mr R. Crook 0454 618181	The sale, hire and service of new and used industrial fork lift trucks

Appx

ORIGINAL ART-SHOPS LTD 12 Southchurch Road Southend on Sea Essex SS1 2NE	Mr M. Francis 0702 460391	Retail of original and reproduced pictures including instant framing
PROFESSIONAL APPEARANCE SERVI-CES LTD 1 Queen Square Bath BA1 2HE	Mr D. Cook 0225 312756	Contract cleaning mainly in the automotive field and commercial premises
SNAPPY SNAPS UK LTD 52 Nottinghill Gate London W11 3HT	Mr T.J. MacAndrews 01 727 6680	1-hour film processing and developing, plus ancillary photographic and retail sales
STAINED GLASS OVERLAY 23 Hurricane Way Norwich NR6 6HE	Mr David Hubbard 0603 485454	Business format franchise involving the design, sale and manufacture of simulated stained glass
TEAM AUDIO LTD Haverscroft Industrial Estate New Road Attleborough Norfolk NR17 1YE	Mr D. Fossey 0953 454544	Wholesale distribution of home electronics equipment and accessories by mobile showroom
TRUST PARTS LTD Unit 7 Groundwell Industrial Estate Crompton Road Swindon Wilts SN2 5AY	Mr R. Wilson 0793 723749	Van sales of workshop consumables and allied products
VENTROLLA LTD 51 Tower Street Harrogate N. Yorks HG1 1HS	Mr R.W. Tunnicliffe 0423 67004	Patented draught proofing system to windows and doors including fitting of security locks
WEIGH & SAVE 3rd Floor Bridgewater House Whitmarsh Street Manchester M1 6LU	Mrs C. Amos 061 236 7374	Sale of non-branded loose dried foodstuffs weighed out by the customer from hygienically sealed bulk drums

Note from Director

It should be borne in mind that, although franchising substantially reduces the inherent risk in a new business venture, it does not automatically guarantee success.

At the same time, registration with or membership of this or any other Association does not automatically protect the member company, or his franchisee, against commercial failure.

BFA Administrative Office:
Franchise Chambers
Thames View
Newtown Road
Henley-on-Thames
Oxon RG9 1HG
(0491) 578049

British Franchise Association – Affiliate listing

Solicitors

Adlers 22–26 Paul Street London EC2A 4JH	Martin Mendelsohn Manzoor Ishani	01 481 9100
Bird Semple & Crawford Herron 249 West George Street Glasgow G2 4RB	Malcolm J. Gillies	041 221 7090
Boswell Bigmore 1–3 Wine Office Court Fleet Street London EC4A 3BY	David Bigmore	01 353 3344
Brodies 15 Atholl Crescent Edinburgh EH3 8HA	Mr J.C.A. Voge	031 228 3777
Field Fisher & Martineau Lincoln House 296–302 High Holborn London WC1V 7JL	Mark Abell	01 831 9161

Appx

Forsyte Kerman 79 New Cavendish Street London W1M 8AQ	R.D. Thornton	01 637 8566
Howard Jones & **Company** 32 Market Street Hoylake Wirral Merseyside	Mr G.E. Howard Jones	051 632 3411
MacRoberts 152 Bath Street Glasgow G2 4TB	Michael Bell	041 332 9988
Mundays Speer House 40 The Parade Claygate Esher Surrey	Ray Walley Partner	Esher 67272
Needham & James Windsor House Temple Row Birmingham B2 5LF	John H. Pratt	021 200 1188
Owen White Johnson House Browells Lane Feltham Middx TW13 7EQ	Anton Bates	01 890 0505
Peters & Peters 2 Harewood Place Hanover Square London W1R 9HB	Raymond Cannon	01 629 7991
Stephenson Harwood One St Pauls Churchyard London EC4M 8SH	Mr J. Schwarz	01 329 4422

Chartered accountants

Arthur Young Rolls House 7 Rolls Buildings Fetter Lane London EC4A 1NH	Andy Pollock Richard Findlater	01 831 7130
BDO Binder Hamlyn Ballantine House 168 West George Street Glasgow G2 2PT	Mr C.R.J. Foley	01 353 3020
KPMG Peat Marwick McLintock Aquis Court 31 Fishpool Street St Albans Herts AL3 4RF	Mr G. Hopkinson	0727 43000
Kidsons Carlton House 31–34 Railway Street Chelmsford Essex CM1 1NJ	Mr D.V. Collins	0245 269595
Levy Gee Consultants Ltd 11 Chalk Farm Road London NW1 8EH	Mr Graham J. Woolfman	01 267 4477
Neville Russell 246 Bishopsgate London EC2M 4PB	Mr John Chastney	0603 617009
Price Waterhouse Southwark Towers 32 London Bridge Street London SE1 9SY	Mr W. Clark	01 407 8989
Spicer & Oppenheim Friary Court 65 Crutched Friars London EC3N 2NP	Nigel Moorland	01 480 7766

Appx

| Touche Ross
Hill House
1 Little New Street
London EC4A 3TR | Mr M.A.B. Jenks | 01 353 8011 |

Exhibition organizers

| Blenheim Princedale Ltd
Blenheim House
137 Blenheim Crescent
London W11 | Neville Buch | 01 727 1929 |

Media and communications

CGB Publishing Newspaper House Tannery Lane Penketh Ches WA5 2UD	Mr C.G. Bradbury Publishers of *Business Franchise Magazine*	092572 4234
Franchise World James House 37 Nottingham Road London SW17 7EA	Mr R. Riding	01 767 1371
Murray Maltby Walker & West Belmont House 20 Wood Lane Headingly Leeds LS6 2AE	Mr G. Peacock	0532 744447

Chartered surveyors

| The Griffin Webster
Partnership
163 West George Street
Glasgow G2 2JJ | David Griffin | 041 248 7808 |
| Stewart Newiss
77 St Vincent Street
Glasgow G2 5TF | Mr J.F. Smith | 041 226 4061 |

Taylor Placks 28 South Molton Street London W1Y 1QA	Mr M. Placks	01 629 4456

Bankers

Bank of Scotland plc 57/60 Haymarket London SW1Y 4QY	C.M. Dow	01 925 0499
Barclays Bank plc Corporate Marketing Dept Ground Floor 168 Fenchurch Street London EC3P 3HD	J.S. Perkins	01 283 8989
Clydesdale Bank plc PO Box 43 30 St Vincent Place Glasgow G12 2HL	A.K. Denholm	041 248 7070
Lloyds Bank plc Franchise Unit Small Business Services Mezzanine Floor 71 Lombard Street London EC3P 3BS	A.D. Pope	01 626 1500
Midland Bank plc Mariner House Pepys Street London EC3N 4DA	Ray Hook Julian Moore	01 260 8859 01 260 7951
Natwest Bank plc **Retail Banking Services** **Franchise Section** 2nd Floor 75 Cornhill London EC3V 3NN	P.D. Stern R.L. Leach J.W. Sheppard A.J. Ellingham	01 280 4262 01 280 4263 01 280 4596 01 280 4264
The Royal Bank of **Scotland plc** PO Box 348 42 Islington High Street London N1 8XL	A.K.C. Auld	01 833 2121

Appx

| The Royal Bank of | R. Campbell | 031 556 8555 |

The Royal Bank of
Scotland plc
42 St Andrew Square
Edinburgh EH2 2YE
    R. Campbell   031 556 8555

TSB Scotland plc
Henry Duncan House
P.O. Box 177
120 George Street
Edinburgh EH2 4TS
    R.G. KcKie   031 225 4555

Patent and trade mark agents

Ladas & Parry
52–54 High Holborn
London WC1V 6RR
    Iain C. Baillie   01 242 5566
    264255 LAWLAN G

Member New York Bar and UK Chartered Patent and Trademark Agent.
International franchise law and intellectual property (e.g. trademarks,
copyright) law.

Insurance brokers

Tolson Messenger Ltd
148 King Street
London W6 0QU
    Mr T.C. Fletcher   01 741 8361

Financial services

Franchise Finance Ltd
Holdhurst
Sutton Place
Abinger
Surrey RH5 6RL
    Mrs S. Kerr   0306 730294

Franchise consultants

Caledonian Franchise
Consultants
Hilltop House
24 Cairnmuir Road
Edinburgh EH12 6LP
    Mr Andrew James   031 334 8040

Caltain Associates Bridlepath House Broken Gate Lane Denham Bucks UB9 4LB	Mr R.W. Crook	0895 834200
Corporate Franchising & **Licensing** Brent House Radford Road Crawley W. Sussex RH10 3NW	Mr John Gooderham	0293 884106
Franchise & Marketing **Management** 46/48 Thornhill Road Streetly Sutton Coldfield W. Midlands B74 3EH	Mr M. Matthews	021 353 0031/2
Saffery Champness **Consultancy Services Ltd** Orchard Court Whaddon Lane Owslebury Winchester Hants SO21 1JJ	Mr Derek Ayling	0962 74544 0202 294281 London office: 01 405 2828
Stoy Hayward **Franchising Services** 8 Baker Street London W1M 1DA	David Acheson	01 486 5888

Appx

Index

Fill the gaps in your NatWest Small Business Bookshelf!

The books in the NatWest Small Business Bookshelf contain all you need to know about managing your small business. Written in a concise, readable style, each book is a handy and authoritative reference on important aspects of small business management.

Titles in the NatWest Small Business Bookshelf are:

A Business Plan
Alan West
A guide for strategic planning for profit. Evaluates key areas and includes case studies and spreadsheets

Starting Up
Gary Jones
How to find ideas for new enterprises and build up to a successful start-up

Selling
Peter Allen
How to understand customers and cashflow, choose your market position and sell correctly

Hiring and Firing
Karen Lanz
How to recruit, manage, pay and part with staff effectively and within the law

Small Business Survival
Roger Bennett
How to manage operational matters more effectively and turn your business into a profitable venture

Retailing
Gary Jones
How to open and run a shop of any sort effectively and profitably

Managing Growth
Maureen Bennett
A guide for the business on the brink of major expansion, focusing on resources management, finance and leadership

Book-keeping and Accounting
Geoffrey Whitehead
A guide for the small trader which looks at simple bookkeeping systems, and explains business accounts, ratios and other performance indicators

Exporting
James Dudley
How to plan for export marketing, new markets and sell profitably overseas

Franchising
Peter Hall and Rob Dixon
A guide for both the business owner seeking to franchise a business and the would-be franchisor

Titles in the NatWest Small Business Bookshelf are available from all good bookshops. In case of difficulty, contact the publisher.

Sales Department, Pitman Publishing, 128 Long Acre, London WC2E 9AN
Tel: 01 379 7383